TEACHING, LEARNING, AND THE HOLOCAUST

Scholarship of Teaching and Learning

Jennifer Meta Robinson
Whitney M. Schlegel
Mary Taylor Huber
Pat Hutchings
editors

TEACHING, LEARNING, AND THE HOLOCAUST

AN INTEGRATIVE APPROACH

HOWARD TINBERG & RONALD WEISBERGER

Indiana University Press
Bloomington and Indianapolis

This book is a publication of

Indiana University Press
Office of Scholarly Publishing
Herman B Wells Library 350
1320 East 10th Street
Bloomington, Indiana 47405 USA

iupress.indiana.edu

Telephone orders   800-842-6796
Fax orders   812-855-7931

Library of Congress Cataloging-in-Publication Data

Tinberg, Howard B., [date]
   Teaching, learning, and the Holocaust : an integrative
approach / Howard Tinberg and Ronald Weisberger.
     pages cm. — (Scholarship of teaching and learning)
     Includes index.
     ISBN 978-0-253-01132-9 (cl : alk. paper) — ISBN 978-0-253-01133-6
(pb : alk. paper) — ISBN 978-0-253-01146-6 (eb) 1. Holocaust, Jewish
(1939-1945)—Study and teaching. I. Weisberger, Ronald. II. Title.
     D804.33.T56 2013
     940.53'18071—dc23

                                                          2013022244

1 2 3 4 5   19 18 17 16 15 14

For my mother and father,
who began from the ashes—and for
the grandparents, uncles, aunts, and cousins
whom I never knew
HT

For those relatives left in the "old world"
and those who survived in the "new"
to carry on the memory of our ancient tradition
RW

We speak in their stead, by proxy.
Primo Levi, "Shame"

CONTENTS

Preface   ix

Acknowledgments   xv

Introduction   1

1 ▪ Contexts   10

2 ▪ Discipline   25

3 ▪ What We Knew and When We Knew It   40

4 ▪ Bystanders and Agents   51

5 ▪ Witnesses   61

6 ▪ Trauma   75

7 ▪ Reclaiming Faith   90

Appendix A: Course Syllabus   109

Appendix B: Reading Journal Template   117

Appendix C: Critical Research Project   119

Appendix D: Midterm and Final Exams   123

Works Cited   125

Index   131

PREFACE

Ever since the publication of Ernest Boyer's *College: The Undergraduate Experience*, and particularly *Scholarship Reconsidered*, the idea that research on teaching and learning could be a legitimate form of scholarship has been debated in the academy. The scholarship of teaching and learning, often referred to as SoTL, looks to the classroom as a rich source of knowledge. Sadly, SoTL has not always been given the same prestige or recognition as other forms of research. It was the goal of *Scholarship Reconsidered* "to move beyond the 'teaching versus research' debate and give scholarship a broader, more efficacious meaning" (Glassick, Huber, and Maeroff ix). Although strides have been made in recognizing SoTL, it still often lacks the backing of committees on tenure and promotion, particularly in baccalaureate and traditional research institutions.

Those of us teaching at community colleges face additional hurdles. In these institutions teaching is supposed to be the main function of the faculty. However, one of the main obstacles to SoTL at two-year schools is a bias against research, *even if that research includes teaching as its subject*. In fact, spending precious time reflecting on one's teaching in an organized and disciplined way and sharing such knowledge through conferences and publications are often seen as luxuries. The majority of instructors in such schools do not see themselves as researchers nor are they viewed as such by administrators. We believe that teaching separated from reflective practice and collegial exchange runs the risk of stultification and that community college faculty who are afforded little time, few resources, and only nominal recognition to engage in scholarly reflection will see their own professional identities as knowledge makers diminished—in essence, they are becoming mere delivery systems. In this age of proliferating online instruction (including freely dispensed fare such as massive open online courses), such a threat is no longer merely an abstraction.

The situation at public community colleges has worsened as state and federal budget cuts have decreased the number of full-time instructors, thus increasing the burden of full-time faculty in the form of increased committee work and other administrative functions. Faculty at many community colleges are now teaching five or more courses, making it even more difficult to do necessary research. Often they work alone, with little opportunity to share their experience with colleagues. The majority of teaching is now done by adjunct faculty, who clearly have little time to do classroom research as they struggle to just make a living teaching in a variety of institutions that give them little support.

Even as public colleges have seen funding decreases, faculty have experienced increased pressure to assess what they are doing and to push for higher completion rates, particularly at community colleges. One way, of course, to facilitate retention and increase graduation is to promote excellence in teaching, a fact that brings us to the scholarship of teaching and learning. It is only through organized inquiry, reflection, and critical exchange—all hallmarks of SoTL—that we can determine which forms of pedagogy work best. Two year–college faculty have an advantage over their four-year peers in that classes tend to be much smaller—and, although students who come from diverse backgrounds may be more challenging, that very diversity makes them rich subjects for scholarly inquiry.

Those teaching at two-year institutions also have an advantage over their four-year colleagues in that community college faculty face less pressure to engage in specific disciplinary research and thus have opportunities to do the type of research promoted by SoTL. Fortunately, despite tight budgets and ambivalence toward research as a teaching-focused activity, there has been some important movement toward sharing information about teaching. At our college, for example, we were able to obtain a large grant to establish a center for teaching and learning. The center was retained after the end of the grant and remains a place where faculty can come together to share ideas and engage in classroom research across the curriculum. During the life of our grant, a journal was published, helping to facilitate the exchange of pedagogical ideas across disciplines. It was discontinued due to fiscal constraints, but we hope that it will be revived. Meanwhile, faculty at two-year colleges continue to engage in and facilitate scholarly conversations. Howard was the editor of a peer-reviewed national journal, *Teaching English at the Two-Year College,* which remains an important venue for the exchange of scholarly reflection on teaching in English. Other subject areas boast their own scholarly forums. Now online sites such as blogs make this sort of exchange easier—and, of course, less expensive—than in the past.

Another development fostering SoTL at two-year institutions, as well as four-year colleges, is the acceptance of learning communities. These arrangements promote integrative learning, facilitate critical learning, and promote cross-disciplinary discussion among faculty. Yet it should also be noted that learning communities offer two year–college faculty perhaps the first opportunity since graduate school to examine their own assumptions as to what it means to do work in their own disciplines. Such realizations are likely to occur, we have found, when faculty engage in conversations with colleagues outside their own disciplines.

For students in learning communities, the payoff is rich indeed. Students become part of a supportive cohort, and at the same time gain an appreciation both of the nature of disciplinary thinking and of the interconnectedness among varied disciplines—such as English and psychology or astronomy and mathematics.

Such interconnectedness is the subject of this book, in which we describe our efforts to integrate two subjects in one course, in this case literature and history. Although challenges (in part budgetary) to instituting learning communities across the curriculum still exist, the rewards for doing so are great. Studies have shown that learning communities help to promote retention and critical thinking (Engstrom and Tinto). They also promote, as we have suggested, intense faculty conversations about the disciplines and the connections between them. This occurs in the planning stage, in which conversations are both rich and complex, but also in the ongoing process as the course proceeds.

The connection between learning communities and SoTL is clear. Learning communities provide a wonderful opportunity and a rich source of research material for classroom research. Written assignments as well as examinations can be discussed among participating colleagues and sharp assessments made of student work. Of course, for such work to be a scholarly product that expands our understanding of teaching and learning, we must establish a clear process for conducting and assessing the research. As Glassick, Huber, and Maeroff point out in regard to acceptable research, "All works of scholarship . . . involve a common sequence of unfolding stages" (24). These stages are comprised of the following elements:

1. Clear goals
2. Adequate preparation
3. Appropriate methods
4. Significant results
5. Effective presentation
6. Reflective critique (25)

In conducting our research project, which has resulted in this work, we have tried to follow these guidelines.

We have long believed that the classroom is a fertile field for the scholarship of teaching. Both of us have been involved in SoTL workshops, presenting papers and leading discussions based on our own and others' classroom practices for a number of years. We have individually and jointly written papers on topics related to classroom research. For many years, as has been noted, Howard was the editor of a peer-reviewed national journal, *Teaching English at the Two-Year College,* and has written or collaborated on a number of books related to teaching English across the disciplines. He was also a fellow with the Carnegie Academy for the Scholarship of Teaching and Learning (CASTL), where he was able to do a preliminary study that has been integrated into the present work. We taught the honors course "Remembering the Holocaust in Literature and History" for eight years before embarking on the research project that culminated in this book. During that time we have had numerous discussions about the course and have made a number of changes in regard to the books to be read, topics covered, and the types of assignments we wanted our students to do. The influence of this productive conversation is evident in the work.

As we make clear throughout the book, we believe in the importance of teaching about the Holocaust. It is a subject that can help to foster not only critical thinking but an appreciation of diversity and a standard of morality among students. We also believe strongly in conducting classroom research so as to further our knowledge of the most effective classroom practices. We believe that the community college is an important arena in which to do so and thus assist instructors at all levels of academia to be better practitioners. Knowledge of all kinds is cumulative. While we do not make any claims to having made a major breakthrough in our understanding of teaching and learning, we do hope that this work can play a part in furthering our understanding of how our students learn and how our instructors can best teach.

ACKNOWLEDGMENTS

We wish to thank the many students who have, over the years, taken up the challenge of studying the Holocaust with us, especially those students whose words and works appear in this study. Thanks also go to the faculty, staff, and administration at our college who have supported our efforts to bring Holocaust education to our students—with special thanks to the various directors of our college's honors program, most recently and most notably, Tom Grady. Our students have done the program proud. Finally, and most importantly, we wish to thank the many survivors who have addressed our classes and who have moved us all so deeply.

TEACHING, LEARNING, AND THE HOLOCAUST

Introduction

Teaching as a Scholarly Activity: Posing Pedagogical Questions

In this book we take up the call, articulated by teacher-scholars Deborah Vess and Sherry Linkon, to study the effects of interdisciplinary teaching "on student learning in the context of specific courses" (94). Our goal in part is to reconstruct the Spring 2011 session of a team-taught interdisciplinary course called "Remembering the Holocaust in Literature and History," which we have taught for nearly a decade. In doing so, we hope to make our teaching visible and available for study—by ourselves as well as by those committed to the scholarship of teaching and learning. We harbor no illusions about the challenges ahead. Recreating a course that has since passed into memory poses its own special challenges: How do we capture the ebbs and flows and the spontaneity of the classroom? What artifacts do we provide as representative of the experience? What material do we foreground? What do we leave out? Why? If there is one lesson (among so many) to be learned from teaching the Holocaust it is that memory work (the recollection of a dramatic event) can be exceedingly challenging.

Recollecting a course about the Shoah specifically (we will use the word *Shoah*, a Hebrew term meaning "catastrophe," in reference to the Holocaust from this point forward) places a special burden on us, since so much learning occurs in silent reflection. We learned long ago that teaching the Shoah calls upon what Lee Shulman has termed "pedagogies of interruption" (*Teaching* 57). Whereas Shulman refers to faculty-generated disruption, we hope to amply demonstrate in this book that the subject of the Shoah itself *compels* interruption, whether faculty desire it or not. A student may be called up short when, reading Abraham Lewin's harrowing "Diary of the Great Deportation," she comes upon this passage:

> The 14th day of the "action" . . . is being continued at full speed. . . . The Germans work *together with the Jewish police*. . . . There are stories of terrible lootings and violence during the expulsions. . . . Shops are broken open and the goods carried out. *In this participate Jewish police, ordinary Jewish neighbors* and Germans. (170)

How can that be? Why would Jews willingly collaborate with their persecutors? Such difficult questions often arise in response to reading Shoah material, prompting a pause for hard but important reflection.

For our part, writing this book allows us the reflective space to pose a series of pedagogically based questions that go to the heart of teaching and learning. A course on the Shoah engages students in a visceral way, evoking intensely strong emotions. A challenge for all is to be able to balance the affective response with a critical awareness: How do we encourage or promote a way of understanding the Shoah that integrates the affective and cognitive domains? How do we know that such a balance occurs when we see it? Moreover, given that our course is interdisciplinary in nature—drawing as it does upon the fields of history, literary criticism, and rhetoric—how do we render explicit the discrete ways of knowing associated with each of these fields? How do we inculcate in our students a way of responding to Shoah material that is integrative of all three approaches? How do we assess success in its achievement?

In raising questions that are pedagogically based, we steer clear of tracing course outcomes that extend well beyond the semester's end and cannot be documented with evidence. One Shoah scholar, for example, wonders aloud,

> Do we make better human beings? Do our students develop a sense of human rights? Can a study of the plight of the Jews and others during the Holocaust create empathy for the "other"? (Feinstein 62)

Although we have observed when teaching the Shoah that students are often intensely engaged with the subject, and hear from many that the course was truly memorable for them, we can make no judgment as to a student's "sense of human rights" when they are in our class, nor do we have access to data suggesting whether such a sense occurred well after the fact. Instead, as scholars for whom the classroom provides ready evidence of student transformation and development, we choose to pose questions that are pedagogically based and to derive evidence accessible in the classroom. Moreover, as teacher-scholars trained in the disciplines of English studies (literary criticism, rhetoric and composition) and history, we choose to draw upon methods of collecting and analyzing evidence that are characteristic of those disciplines.

Points of Inquiry

Like most veteran teachers, we know a good problem when we see one. Over the ten years that we have taught our interdisciplinary honors seminar on the Shoah we have engaged in a good deal of problem posing, which, as Randy Bass and Lee Shulman have argued, can be fertile ground for research and knowledge building in the classroom (Bass; Shulman, *Teaching* 59). From the start, we have been eager to achieve the following goals in this course: to model the ways of thinking characteristic of history and English studies, and at the same time to promote—through classroom discussion and written prompts—an approach to the subject that was integrative of the disciplines. Rather than seeing these goals as contradictory, we see interdisciplinarity itself as requiring a self-conscious deployment of disciplinary practices. "The basis of any interdisciplinary study," write Vess and Linkon, "is an examination of disciplinary methodologies and perspectives, and . . . 'the worldview and underlying assumptions of each discipline must be made explicit'" (91). Our job, then, requires that we render those assumptions explicit and expect students to engage in the hard work of the disciplines. After all, the disciplines continue to make knowledge building possible. Indeed, according to Timothy Lenoir, "Disciplines are institutionalized formations for organizing schemes of perception, appreciation, and action, and for inculcating them as tools of cognition and communication" (72). We simply cannot do without them. We are, as some have noted, "disciplined by our disciplines" (Messer-Davidow, Shumway, and Sylvan vii).

That said, we recognize the changing landscape of the academy—notably, the increasing popularity of interdisciplinary work (Huber and Hutchings 68; Klein 77). When we took up the challenge of designing and then teaching an interdisciplinary seminar on the Shoah, we confronted the daunting task not only of studying the most heinous crime of the twentieth century but also of constructing a model of teaching that neither of us had ever seen in action: a truly interdisciplinary course that attempts to elucidate and synthesize our disciplines and our teaching styles. We were after a symbiosis for which we possessed no map. This book might, then, be seen as the first step toward creating that map—for ourselves and for others who wish to embark on this journey. To that end, we wish to pose and probe the following questions:

- How do we promote students' understanding of disciplinary methods and perspectives?
- What are the obstacles faced by students, especially community college students, in replicating disciplinary approaches?
- How do we measure disciplinary understanding?
- How might we effectively promote a synthesis of disciplinary practices and ways of knowing in our students' work?
- How do we measure that synthesis?
- What difficulties do students experience when attempting to work between and across disciplines (resulting in "cognitive dissonance," according to Vess and Linkon 100)?

When we initially designed and then taught the course, we respected the separation between our disciplines. Each of us ordered texts representative of our fields: a narrative history of the Shoah and an anthology of Shoah literature. In that first iteration of the course, essay exams typically had a question focusing on history and a question requiring literary or rhetorical analysis. Class sessions were divided evenly between history and English. The history professor lectured on matters of historical fact; the English professor led discussions on the literature. It seemed, in those early days, to be two courses pretending to be one.

Over the years, we have worked hard to understand each other's disciplinary practices and to model a synthesis of those practices for our students. Instead of dividing class sessions in half, we routinely engage in cross talk throughout the session. Instead of posing exam questions that segregate disciplines, we now compose prompts that explicitly embrace our disciplines and call upon students to demonstrate a facility with both, as in this example from a midterm exam:

> The study of the Shoah, some have argued, begins at the intersection of memory and historical documentation. In other words, what we know of the Shoah is the product both of human memory and the historical record left by perpetrators and victims. In a clear and thoughtful essay, write about the contribution that each—memory and the historical record—plays. We suggest that you begin with definitions: What is memory? What is fact? In the study of the Shoah, where do the two converge? Where do they diverge or differ? Then proceed to compose an essay that refers in detail to at least TWO of the works that we have read so far, one being our history text and the other drawn from the literature. You may, in addition, make use of the testimony that we have heard.

While we preserve distinctions between history texts and literature, we call upon students to work at the intersection of disciplines—in this case of historical fact and recollection of the past through memory. As the prompting suggests, we want students to attend both to convergence and divergence—to interdisciplinarity and to distinctions between disciplines.

In Spring 2011, after seven years of careful thought and collegial exchanges about our course, we felt prepared to undertake a systematic study of what students learn in our course, how they learn it, and how we know that they learn it. We had also acquired a self-reflexivity about our own teaching that we wished to test against the evidence of the course itself: Have we truly managed to make the pedagogical moves necessary to model disciplinary and interdisciplinary practices? How do we know? To further motivate us to study the course, we were eager to understand the effect of a significant course revision. That spring, we required that students read a collection of interpretive essays rather than a straightforward narrative history of the Shoah. And in the process we organized the syllabus not chronologically but thematically, engaging students for the first time to think about such complex subjects as faith after Auschwitz, the role of the Church during the war, and Shoah denial. Although we would not have a control group with which to compare our students, we were nonetheless anxious to determine what students gained from these changes: would they likely, for example, achieve an interpretive and speculative stance on aspects of the Shoah rather than a response based solely on reporting the facts?

Method

This book reports on a naturalistic study of a single class in a single semester. In conducting such a study, we follow in the footsteps of many in composition who, in Bonnie Sundstein's phrase, "assume the responsibility for studying people inside their cultural surroundings" (178). Ethnographies of the classroom, or qualitative studies that focus on learning as expressed through written texts, have figured prominently in composition studies for decades. From the groundbreaking work of James Britton and Janet Emig, who studied the literacies of adolescent writers; to the rich ethnographies of community literacies conducted by Shirley Brice Heath, Anne Gere, Deborah Brandt, and Ellen Cushman; and to the pioneering longitudinal study of student writers at the City College of New York by Marilyn Sternglass, compositionists have endeavored to research student literacies by reading closely the writing and the context that engenders the writing. Our project, following these researchers' leads, will foreground the words of students themselves.

And yet, as Sundstein has noted, ethnographers enter into a "tangled tension—between presentation and representation—between our informants, their texts, ourselves, our texts, and our readers" (178). Our presence as classroom instructors affects what goes on in our classrooms—an influence that needs to be noted. Hence, in this project, we assume a self-reflective stance throughout—telling our stories as well as allowing students, through their words, to tell their own. To that complex purpose, we assembled, with the students' consent, a course and teaching portfolio containing all the documents produced by ourselves and our students: the syllabus, prompts and responses to weekly reading journals, in-class exam questions and essays, and digital snapshots from—and our commentary on—students' culminating research projects. Of course, the writings that faculty and students produce tell only part of the story of what transpires in a semester-long course. What of the class give and take? How might that be rendered and studied? To achieve that end, we recorded—again with the students' consent—entire class sessions. Although constrained by limited resources, we were nonetheless able to have a portion of those sessions transcribed. We are guided in the reading of all these texts by our research questions: What evidence do we see of a nascent disciplinary knowledge? Where do we begin to see a synthesis of disciplines? What obstacles to such understanding do we note?

Overview of the Book

To lay the groundwork for the analysis to come, chapter 1 provides institutional and personal contexts. We begin with an account of how we came to the college and how we came to teach a course on the Shoah. Like our students' journeys to the classroom, the paths that we took to become Shoah educators were hardly predictable and routine. We then offer a brief history of the college, describe its mission, and analyze student demographics. Noting the particular nature of the honors program, its students, and its own discrete mission, we lay out our course objectives and desired outcomes.

Chapter 2 operates from the assumption, as noted by Lee Shulman, that teaching and learning are "domain-specific" (Foreword vi). In other words, the disciplinary practices and conventions that we bring to the classroom matter. In this chapter, we render those methods and expectations explicit, addressing questions such as these: What does it mean to render the past as a historian? How does a critic read and write about a poem or short story? What does a rhetorical analysis of nonfiction prose look like? What constitutes evidence in history and English studies? What ways of thinking underlie work in these disciplines? Not surprisingly, given that we undertook distinctively different disciplinary training, our teaching styles differ as well. We note those differences but also comment on the ways that our teaching styles, like our disciplinary methods, have undergone cross-fertilization over the ten years of teaching the course. The chapter concludes with commentary on that synthesis of disciplinary and teaching styles, as well as the integration of affect and cognition in reading Shoah material.

Chapter 3 accounts for what students bring to the course, as well as our own knowledge, at the start. We explore what students know about the Shoah and how they came to know it. We trace our own development as learners about the Shoah—self-trained, essentially, since neither of us studied the Shoah formally before setting out to teach the course for the first time. This chapter also delineates the class structure and gives a rationale for its organization. Included in this discussion of structure will be a statement of theory as to how students develop over time an understanding of the complex course content.

Chapter 4 deploys a critical element in Shoah studies—the distinction between a bystander and an actor or agent—as a lens through which to view student interaction in the classroom. After defining these terms and their significance for the Shoah and for instruction, we draw upon class transcripts, reading journals, and formal writing to concretize these categories and answer the following questions: In what sense might students be seen as bystanders? What was said or written and in what context? By contrast, what constitutes active student learning in the course? Where is the evidence of agency? How do we problematize these terms? In other words, how might students demonstrate agency through silence and reflection? We will also examine our own position as instructors along a "bystander–agent" spectrum. To what extent are we directive as teachers? When or how do we stand back to allow student development?

"Above all, we need the witness," writes the historian Yehuda Bauer. "There is no Holocaust history without witnesses" ("Explicable" 23). Chapter 5 considers the role of the witness when studying the Shoah. Drawing upon current Shoah scholarship (and the pioneering work of Lawrence Langer) as well as an analysis of video and live testimony given during the course and student response to that testimony, this chapter places the witness front and center. This chapter includes classroom discussion on the relationship between memory work and historical research—between witness testimony and scholarly history—and also documents students' growing understanding of the role of testimony in understanding the Shoah.

Students who take Shoah courses inevitably become intensely engaged with the material, especially with readings and media that represent atrocity and trauma. Chapter 6 documents the pedagogical choices that we made to anticipate such emotional reactions and the responses of our students to those choices. We note, specifically, our decision not to show graphic images of atrocity unmediated. Even so, the reactions among our students to reading, say, Abraham Lewin's "The Diary of the Great Deportation" or Jan T. Gross's *Neighbors* are quite intense and difficult for students to manage. For many, as a result, critical awareness shuts down. This chapter, then, first documents and analyzes students' response to the literature and history of trauma. It then points to ways of promoting a balance between emotion and critique, between the affective and the cognitive response to such material. Finally, we narrate our own personal struggles when reading Shoah texts.

In Chapter 7 we look closely at, and document, what we and our students have learned by the end of the course. We are assisted in this process by the students themselves, whose culminating research projects in the form of digital snapshots (web-based electronic posters) focus on an essential question. More precisely, we offer evidence of students' acquisition of new knowledge and of the knowledge that has been replaced. We, too, reflect on our own learning and unlearning during the course, personally and pedagogically. Finally, we consider the lessons learned from ten years of engaging this most challenging of subjects.

1 ▪ Contexts

It shows me that Nazis were men, just as we are now.
Michael, reading journal, February 2011

Like the historian Paul Bartrop, we came to study and teach
the Shoah "from somewhere else" (1). In some sense the phrase "from
somewhere else" serves as an apt metaphor or trope for the journeys
that each of us took to get to the Shoah classroom. Like the paths of so
many of our students, whose experiences are often marked by aspira-
tions checked by stark reality and the subsequent recalibration and
adjustments, our journey to the present was hardly linear or predictable. Neither of us, for example, had intended from the start to teach
at a community college, nor did either of us expect to teach a course
on the Shoah, given our prior academic training as a historian and as a
scholar in British Romanticism. Far from anticipating an opportunity
to teach the Shoah, we regarded the Shoah, for our own personal reasons, as a subject to avoid. Indeed, the subject presented genuine risks
for one of us, a child of Shoah survivors.

"From somewhere else": as we continue to think through the
implications of that phrase, we note another aspect that strikes home.
Even before undertaking the challenges of teaching a subject in which
we had received no explicit training in graduate school, each of us had
undertaken retraining of a different sort. In one case, it was the shift
from teaching literature (British Romanticism, precisely) exclusively
to teaching composition and rhetoric as well as directing a writing
center. In the other case, it was the shift from serving as history faculty
exclusively to studying developmental theory as applied to adult learn-

ers and becoming director of academic tutoring. Yes, we have come from somewhere else.

Howard Tinberg's Narrative

"*Sha, shtil* [be quiet]": I heard these Yiddish words often as a young child. I assumed then that my parents were simply reminding my siblings and me to mind our manners. In later years, I would see these two words as emblematic of my parents' predicament: quietly suffering Jewish refugees who lost just about all their relatives—both sets of parents, siblings, cousins, uncles, and aunts—during the Shoah. I had not fully realized the import of those words until as an adult I read this passage from Alan Dershowitz's memoir, *Chutzpah:*

> I am a proud and assertive Jew, and a proud and assertive American. Many in my generation no longer feel like guests in anyone else's land. It is not enough for us, as it was for our grandparents and parents, that we be tolerated as a minority in a country where only the majority are first-class citizens. We insist on being treated as equals. We have no qualms about seeing a Goldberg, a Shapiro, or a Cohen run for governor or even president. We need not *sha shtil* (be quiet) as my grandmother constantly warned. We don't have to worry about *shande far di goyim* or being "lightening rods" for anti-Semitism if we are too visible or successful. Maybe we are overconfident. Maybe we are no more secure than the Jews of Germany thought they were in 1929. Maybe we are tempting fate—and history—by our assertiveness. Again, as my grandmother would say, *Keyn ayn hore,* I hope not. And I don't think so. (19–20)

Reading this passage conveyed to me this unmistakable message: my parents, as a result of being singled out for destruction during the Shoah because they were Jews, wanted us all to remain under the radar. Calling attention to ourselves might bring terrible consequences. My family, as a result, did not exhibit the kind of *chutzpah*—brazenness— that Dershowitz claims proudly. We had lost too much.

My parents, both deceased, had not burdened us as we were growing up with stories from the war. Late in life, as is typical of Shoah survivors, my mother wanted to share as much as she could of what she knew from her past life during the war. This much my siblings and I have been able to construct, from my mother's account—our chief source of facts, although, as the citations indicate, I have begun to flesh out details of my mother's narrative and will continue to do so throughout this book: My mother grew up on a small, rural village—a shtetl, or collection of farms—in eastern Poland (now Ukraine), in a place called Jablonka, forty-three miles southwest of Krakow. Nestled in a small valley, Jablonka consisted of three streets, which, according to a former resident, "resembles an eagle, and since nearby was the river Raczka Jablon (and from this derived the name of town Jablonka), the shtetl had the image of an eagle landing from the heights to drink fresh and pure waters" (Wajsbord). According to a census taken in 1911, over 80 percent of the residents were Jewish; ten years later the number would decline to a little over 60 percent ("Jablonka Koscielna"). During the first two decades of the century residents numbered only in the hundreds ("Jablonka Koscielna"). Zionist ideals (supportive of the establishment of a Jewish state) were strong in the village, as was religious observance (Wajsbord). In contrast, my father was raised in Tarnow, forty-five miles east of Krakow. Before World War II Tarnow had some twenty-five thousand residents, half of whom were Jews ("Tarnow"). Rather than relying on farming, Jewish residents worked in clothing manufacturing and were quite diverse—even secular—in regards to religious identification ("Tarnow"). At various points, this part of the country—Galicia—became annexed into Russia, Germany, and Poland.

I suppose that my parents' war experience may also be characterized by the phrase "somewhere else," since they managed to avoid being deported and moved to a concentration or death camp. They were able to elude the Nazis, who were out to kill them for being Jews, as well as the Russians, who sought to impress my father into the army. Facing these pressures, my parents decided to leave their respective families and homes to live life on the run. Moving eastward, they survived mostly by their wits and, according to my mother's telling, her ability to pass as a non-Jew and her talents as a seamstress. But she also worked to dig trenches and in coal mines. One particularly harrowing episode occurred on the Russian side after my father had been ordered to go back home in order to fight the war for the Poles. To join my father, my mother would have to cross a bridge over a river without being detected by the soldiers, who were standing guard. A fellow Jew offered to help her cross over in his hay wagon. Here's how my mother told the story:

> A Jewish guy, a communist, said, "Why don't you climb into that wagon in the hay. I'll cover you all up. Nobody will see you and [I'll] bring you over the bridge." . . . I did and we start going over the bridge. The soldiers came in with their bayonets and stick them there. I feel it. I didn't scream. Finally, he took me over the bridge. (Tinberg, "Personal")

My father had not been drafted into the Russian army. My mother and he resumed their life together, growing their own food in a garden provided by a protector (who also employed my mother, as well as my father). They stayed for the duration of the war, making certain to be inconspicuous.

At the war's end, any thoughts of returning to either Jablonka or Tarnow were dismissed when, according to my mother, news was received that all members of the family had been killed. My parents found their way to a displaced persons camp in Germany, where my two brothers were born. In 1949, the family immigrated to the United States; they were sponsored by my mother's uncle, who had escaped Europe before the war. And so they began life anew, no doubt heartbroken and—despite having started a family—so very much alone.

Strangely enough, as I was growing up, I never thought of my parents as survivors. They did not have numbers tattooed on their arms, after all. Were my parents survivors, although they hadn't been in the camps? The fact is that most survivors indeed never set foot in the camps. Those who entered the camps were not likely to leave them alive, given Nazi efficiency. The "true" survivors were those fortunate enough to have escaped the Nazi trap.

When I was a child, my parents said little to us about the war. I've since learned, from authors such as Helen Epstein and Eva Hoffman, that Shoah survivors rarely talked about their war experiences in the years immediately following. The memories that I had of the Shoah, were, in Marianne Hirsch's well-known term, remnants of "post-memory," after-the-fact bits of information obtained from unknown sources. Eva Hoffman, a child of survivors, describes the phenomenon this way:

> The Holocaust, in my first, childish reception, was a deeply internalized but strangely unknown past. It has become routine to speak of the "memory" of the Holocaust, and to adduce to this faculty a moral, even a spiritual value. But it is important to be precise: We who came after do not have memories of the Holocaust. Even from my most intimate proximity I could not form "memories" of the Shoah or take my parents' memories as my own. Rather, I took in that first information as a sort of fairy tale deriving not so much from another world as from the center of the cosmos: an enigmatic but real fable. (6)

"[E]nigmatic but real": the phrase goes to the heart of what I apprehended about the Shoah. I did feel certain, however, that my parents were, well, strange: quiet, exceedingly hard working, but whose ways and whose richly accented speech were so different from those of everyone else's parents. I also knew that I wished to be somewhere else—anywhere else. Being "here" meant being strangely sad and seriously observant of religious practice—obeying strict dietary laws, observing the Sabbath, and attending synagogue regularly.

As a teen, coming of age in California during the 1960s in a kind of dreamy Los Angeles surfing and Hollywood culture, I was hardly alone in trying to break from homely conventions and the strict requirements of realism. Nevertheless, my siblings and I felt the need to fit in even as our generally serious and somewhat private temperaments and work ethic set us apart from friends. For my part, around middle school, I threw myself into my studies and to getting the best grades I possibly could. The message was clear: school and learning mattered a great deal to our parents, although they were themselves uneducated (my mother had no formal education at all). Yet even as I strove to become different from my parents, I shared the value they attached to education for its own sake (as did my siblings, all of whom went on to obtain doctorates), and to hard work (my father would eventually own two tailor shops).

That said, I would choose to study an area that was as far from my parents' experience as could be: English literature. Truth be told, my brother was a strong influence. An English major in college, he brought books into the home—including the complete Yale Shakespeare, which I read in its entirety over the years—thanks to a membership in the Book of the Month club. It is one of many oddities in our home environment that although my parents were self-educated and spent a good deal of time (as we all did) watching television (it was still new when I was a child), reading was encouraged. After all, my mother had been fluent in several languages. And Jewish traditions privileged the reading of the Torah and Biblical commentary. Hence, when my parents purchased the complete *Encyclopedia Britannica,* a glorious event representing a significant financial sacrifice, it was not altogether surprising.

Still, I kept my distance from subjects that seemed to recall my parents' experience—reading little about the Jewish experience and, certainly, about Hitler's war against the Jews. I barely acknowledged bigoted references to Jews in Shakespeare or T. S. Eliot or Charles Dickens when I came across them. I was, after all, somewhere else than where I had started. I imagined myself happily ensconced in academe—teaching Keats or Wordsworth at a respected university, with summers off visiting Wordsworth's home in Grasmere and reciting passages from "The Prelude."

In the coming years, I would confront a far different reality: after a strong undergraduate career at UCLA, but an unsuccessful stint at its graduate school, I needed to decide whether I would continue to pursue a dream of college teaching and, if so, where. In the interim, I began to teach at a vocational college in Los Angeles, providing English grammar training to young women of color preparing to become court reporters in the city. I began to see ways that teaching might serve not only to satisfy my own particular ambitions but perhaps also to help other extremely motivated, if underprepared, students. Although teaching at the community college was not even on my radar yet, this experience—at a place called Southland College, located near Vermont and Western in Los Angeles—was something of a revelation for me.

But I continued to harbor a dream of continuing my graduate work in literature, this time far away from the confines of home (I had commuted between home and school for three of my four years of college and two years of graduate school). What follows might be seen as a Hollywood-movie or simply purely ironic: the university that took me in proved to be Brandeis University, established in 1948 by American Jews for American Jews.

Only twice in my life have I ever felt as if I were not a minority: once on a trip to Israel with my mother, and then during my time at Brandeis. It was as if a great burden was lifted from my shoulders: I would not have to apologize (to myself) for taking time off for Jewish holidays (the college was closed!) or eating certain kinds of foods. I was surrounded by buildings named after Goldbergs or Shapiros. As I look back at this momentous turn, I see that this step represented a move toward acceptance of my family's identity as Jews. In light of this return of sorts, it does not seem to be a stretch that I would eventually teach a course on the Shoah. Brandeis remains a symbolically important place for me: I met my wife at Brandeis, and we were married in a traditional Jewish ceremony there.

But that arc took years to complete, including a wide turn away—a year's stint of teaching (with my wife, Toni) in the People's Republic of China. But the shape of the river was becoming clearer: I turned to composition and rhetoric as my professional home. Moreover, after two years teaching writing at a private university and seeing little hope of obtaining tenure there, I heard of a full-time position opening up at a community college in Massachusetts. I took that job in 1987 and have been there ever since. I teach primarily first-year composition, have directed the college's writing center, and have published articles and books in the very welcoming field of composition.

In 2000, my mother passed away—and with her a firsthand knowledge of a world long gone: the shtetl and the *yiddishkeit* (the Yiddish culture) that shaped that small farming community. Would my mother have been surprised that I and a colleague would be teaching a course on the Shoah? Perhaps not. After all, my wife and I sent our two children to Jewish day schools, partly in the hopes of preserving the tie to traditions. But the Shoah? I wonder, now, whether she would welcome my revisiting that terrible time or regard it as a depressing and somewhat futile effort. After all, she and my father could not afford to think much about the terrible losses that they suffered (or they dared not). They were too busy starting a new life. I would like to think, however, that she would see my efforts to study the Shoah as an obligation fulfilled.

Ronald Weisberger's Narrative

I came to Bristol Community College in 1979 after teaching history at a number of colleges and universities. A child of the '60s, I have had a strong interest in social justice issues in general and education in particular. During the 1970s I was involved in a number of what were considered experimental or alternative institutions of higher education, including the Institute for Open Education and the University Without Walls, which had an important influence on my philosophy of education.

Bristol Community College was my first community college experience and, as it turned out, I have devoted the bulk of my academic career to the institution. My interest in higher education pedagogy was the motivation to return to graduate school at the University of Massachusetts Amherst in the area of teaching and learning, where I earned an Ed.D. in higher education in 1994. In 1985, when the college decided to create a full-time peer tutoring program, I applied and was chosen for the position of coordinator of tutoring because of my diverse experiences in higher education. I have also continued to teach a variety of American and world history courses. At the same time, I have participated in a number of Scholarship of Teaching and Learning initiatives. The opportunity to teach an interdisciplinary honors course on the Shoah seemed to be a natural extension of this interest and experience.

My personal interest and involvement with the subject of the Shoah reflect, in part, my identity as a Jew growing up in the Shoah's aftermath. Born in 1943, I came of age when, to a great extent, the Jewish population was still in shock and disbelief that such a catastrophe could have occurred. Like so many Jews in this country my grandparents had come to the United States as part of the great migration of Eastern European Jews at the end of the nineteenth century and the beginning of the twentieth. My father's parents came from areas in the old Austro-Hungarian Empire, and my mother's from Czarist Russia. I was fortunate to have been able to spend a good amount of time with them as I was growing up. Like many Jewish immigrants, they were involved in small businesses, and—although they had initially settled in different parts of Pennsylvania and New Jersey—by the time I was born they had moved to the resort town of Atlantic City, where I grew up. From the time I was three until I was eight, my parents, brother, and I lived with my mother's parents in an inner-city apartment, and my father's parents lived across town in a rooming house that they owned close to Atlantic City's fabled boardwalk.

The desire of both sets of grandparents had been assimilation, but they clearly retained aspects of their previous culture; for example, they spoke Yiddish in addition to English. For a young boy, my grandparents seemed to be, as Howard indicates, from somewhere else. They had foreign-sounding accents, and my Russian grandfather read the Yiddish daily, the *Forward*, which, with its Hebrew lettering, always appeared to me to be from another world. They spoke Yiddish to each other, especially when they didn't want me to know what they were discussing. If on the rare occasion that they were asked about their life in the Old World, they mentioned the precarious situation of the Jewish population in Czarist Russia; my grandmother was saved from murderous Cossacks because she looked more Russian than Jewish, and my grandfather fled the country in 1905 to keep from being impressed into the army during the Russo-Japanese War. Both sets of grandparents sometimes mentioned relatives who had been left in Europe, but to my recollection little was said about those who were surely lost to the Shoah.

As fully assimilated Jews, my parents had tenuous ties with the old country. They had been educated in this country and, in fact, my father attended the Catholic Duquesne University in the early 1930s. Again, I do not recall my parents discussing the Shoah in regard to lost relatives or any other topic. There seemed to be a clear avoidance of the subject, which must have made an impression on a young child growing up. Even when a family of survivors—including two children close to my age—moved next door, there appeared to be a conspiracy of silence as to what their situation had been. We were told that they had come from Europe to be near relatives who lived in the same apartment complex. When from time to time the mother screamed during the night, it was attributed to a mental problem. Although I was friendly with the two children and spent time in their apartment, I don't recall any mention of what had transpired to bring them to this country. This was not a matter for children, although it is not clear that the topic was brought up often among the adults, either.

My mother's parents were not religious, but my father's were, and they convinced my parents to enroll me in the Yeshiva or Jewish day school, which I attended until the third grade, when the school was forced to close because of a lack of funds. The faculty at the school, like most of the American Jewish population, had pivoted to the support of the newly established state of Israel. Some of our teachers had visited there. We listened to guest speakers who had stories of the exciting developments in that new country. The fact that Israeli soldiers had defeated or held off the armies of invading Arab nations was a source of pride. We were urged to contribute to the United Jewish Appeal and to buy trees that would be planted in our name in Israel. Hebrew was an important part of the curriculum and topics such as the victorious Maccabees, who are celebrated in the Jewish holiday of Hanukkah, and the revolt of Bar Kochba, the leader of the first-century fight against the Romans, were seen as exemplars of the Jewish people. The lesson was clear; we were to think of the Jewish people in heroic terms and not dwell on or consider what had just happened to the six million Jews of Europe.

After the Yeshiva closed, I entered public school and a year later my parents bought a home in Ventnor, a suburb of Atlantic City, a migratory pattern of so many Jews of their generation. This move further distanced me from the ties with the older, first generation of European Jews—many of whom, like my grandparents, were still living in the so-called ghettos of the inner city. My family joined a Reform temple with a heavily Americanized structure and liturgy. Growing up in that atmosphere, I rarely heard mention of the Shoah in my family or among my friends or classmates. At our temple, where I attended Sunday school, we learned some Hebrew and the emphasis again was on Israel and the heroic aspects of Jewish history as well as the Reform Jewish movement. There was no discussion—to my recollection—of what had happened to the Jewish population in Europe a decade or so before. It was also a subject that was pretty much avoided in history classes once I entered middle and high school.

Growing up then in an atmosphere of avoidance of the Shoah, I entered college as a history major in 1961; not surprisingly, the Shoah was not uppermost in my mind as subject of study or concern. As it turned out, 1961 was actually the beginning of a turnabout in the way the Shoah was treated by historians, social scientists, and other intellectuals—and even in popular culture. With the capture of Adolf Eichmann and his subsequent trial and execution, the world began to focus more sharply on what had happened twenty years or so earlier. As Shoah scholar Michael Bernard-Donals points out, "Until the Eichmann Trial, there was a great deal of silence after the Holocaust in the United States" (27). Political scientist and historian Ira Katznelson indicates also that "for the first two decades after the second War, there hardly was a scholarly debate about its comprehensibility, character, causes and meaning" (26). Another historian, Robert Abzug, argues that after World War II most Americans had a pretty simplistic idea of their connection to the Shoah. The United States had been the victor in the war and had helped to liberate and free the remnant of the Jewish population in Europe. After seeing the newsreels of camp victims and the results of the Nuremberg Trial in 1945–46, we essentially put aside the Shoah for the next twenty years.

As a history major taking European and American history courses, I noted that the subject of the Shoah would come up, but it received only passing mention both in lectures and in texts. There were no courses on the Shoah where I attended college as an undergraduate and then a graduate student during the 1960s. In addition, when conducting research for papers and later a master's thesis I never considered writing on the subject. In fact, it was only in the late 1960s that a few historians in this country—such as David Wyman—began to turn their attention to the subject, so there were not many secondary sources available (Abzug 209). The major secondary studies on this subject—by historians such as Yehuda Bauer, Martin Gilbert, and others—would not come until the late 1970s and into the 1980s and 1990s (Bauer, *American Jewry*).

For me the Shoah remained in the background for a number of decades as I pursued an academic career. Although I was always conscious of being Jewish and I eventually returned to attending Jewish services after flirting with Unitarianism as a graduate student, the Shoah was not a subject I thought to emphasize in my teaching, reading, or even research.

To be frank, in retrospect it is hard for me to account for why I had avoided confronting the Shoah more directly. In a sense, the avoidance of the subject so prevalent during the time I was coming of age was certainly an influence. There was also the fear of what I might encounter delving deep into the history of the Shoah. As Ira Katznelson points out, those of us influenced by the ideas of progress and the goodness of humanity have a hard time confronting what Hannah Arendt labeled the "banality of evil." Nevertheless, when Howard asked me if I was willing to co-teach a course with the Shoah as the central topic, I finally decided it was time to come to terms with a subject that I had so long avoided. I knew that no courses on the subject were taught at the college. Even a course on World War II barely mentioned it. My students knew very little about the Shoah beyond, perhaps, what they read in Elie Wiesel's *Night* or saw in *Schindler's List*. As important as these works might be, they did not provide much in the way of context. Moreover, most of the students at our community college are not Jewish and have little or no idea about the Jewish population or Judaism, nor why they had been chosen for annihilation. Despite my reservations and fear, I agreed to embark on what has now been an ten-year voyage of teaching and discovery for our students, Howard, and myself.

The College: A Brief History

"All researchers are positioned by age, gender, race, class, nationality, institutional affiliation, historical-personal circumstance, and intellectual predisposition," writes Elizabeth Chiseri-Strater (115). As part of the background for the discussion in the rest of the book, we aim to provide an account of such affiliation and predisposition. Our personal narratives represent an attempt to position ourselves squarely in this project. A brief glimpse into our institution's history serves to similarly place our students and the college itself.

Bristol Community College (BCC), founded in 1965, is part of the public college and university system in the Commonwealth of Massachusetts. As one of fifteen community colleges spread throughout the state, the college serves an area in southeastern Massachusetts that includes the cities of Fall River, New Bedford, and Attleboro, as well as smaller towns and villages in the district (*Fact Sheet*). Its main campus is located in Fall River, an old mill town that at one time was the largest producer of textile products in the world. This industry left the area many years ago, but the mill buildings—now occupied by retail stores, restaurants, health clinics, and a few artist studios—can still be seen throughout the city. Nevertheless, the city never fully recovered from its industrial loss and unemployment there, as well as in other parts of the area, is higher than many other parts of the state.

The growth in the student population, which now is over 12,000 full- and part-time, created a need for additional campuses. In the 1990s and early 2000s two additional sites were created in New Bedford, an old whaling city, and Attleboro, located in the interior of the college's service area of Bristol County (Bristol Community College, *Fact Sheet*). As is true of many other schools, the onset of the online environment has allowed the college to expand its offerings in that mode as well. Of course, with this growth has come the expansion of the faculty, professional staff, and administration. Although the full-time faculty has grown from the earlier small group of pioneers to the current number of 104, the college, as have many others like it, has depended on part-time instructors. In the last couple of years, there has been close to a 3–1 ratio of part-time to full-time instructors (Bristol Community College, *Fifth-Year Report*). As at other institutions, the number of administrators as well as support staff has grown dramatically. In terms of its top administrators, however, the college has been relatively stable, having had only three presidents and five chief academic officers in its history.

Student Demographics

The college's student population reflects the diversity of ethnic groups living in the area. There are a number of students with English, Irish, French Canadian, and especially Portuguese backgrounds. This latter group makes the area somewhat distinctive; beginning in the 1950s there was substantial immigration to the city from the Azores. Recently, however, there has been an increase in the number of Brazilians, Hispanics, Cambodians, and African Americans. New Bedford also has a large population from Cape Verde. In addition, as is true of many community colleges, there are nearly twice as many women enrolled as men, and nearly 43 percent of the students are over twenty-one years of age (Bristol Community College, *Fact Sheet*).

Like students at many other community colleges, a relatively large percentage are first generation and low income. This is not surprising, since the median income of Fall River residents is $34,236—40 percent less than the average median income in Massachusetts (U.S. Census Bureau). In addition, 20 percent of Fall River households are listed as being below the poverty level, and 33 percent of the city's residents lack a high school diploma (U.S. Census Bureau).

The Honors Program

BCC has a very heterogeneous student body, given its mission. In a bid to attract students who might ordinarily apply directly to a baccalaureate institution, an honors program was established a number of years ago. The Commonwealth Honors Program (CHP) was begun in 2000 and is part of a statewide organization that establishes basic rules for such programs. CHP students and affiliated staff have access to a designated honors space that can be utilized for study or as a seminar room for interdisciplinary courses, such as the one that is the subject of this work. This setting creates a seminar atmosphere that helps to facilitate discussion and emphasizes the importance of the course as a part of the honors program.

Within this institutional and programmatic context, we proposed in 2002 to teach a course called "Remembering the Holocaust in Literature and History: An Honors Interdisciplinary Seminar." The course description, which includes overall objectives, runs thus:

> The Holocaust, or, as it has come to be known, the Shoah, is one of the most horrific events in all of world history. Even more than fifty years after the fact, the world continues to struggle with the enormity of this human catastrophe. Nevertheless, a body of writing—both historical and literary—exists that enables us to

confront this key moment in world history. This course serves as an introduction to this work. Students gain an understanding of the historical facts, including circumstances leading up to the Holocaust itself and the event's critical aftermath. In addition, students reflect on the role of literature, principally through accounts of that time written by survivors and the children of survivors, in the struggle to represent an event that many have described as beyond the limits of language to capture.

The course is meant to be introductory, although the bar is raised high, as we note throughout this book. We worried, and continue to worry, about the place of such a course in an institution that focuses on general education and includes students for whom a college education is seen as having practical application toward obtaining jobs and career skills. Myrna Goldenberg has argued, convincingly, that it is precisely at an institution such as ours, with its emphasis on general education, that Shoah education is most appropriate. Community colleges, whose students number about half of all undergraduates, provide splendid opportunities to reach a maximum number of students. But Goldenberg favors a modular approach to Shoah education, embedding a unit on the Shoah in general education courses such as history. Ours is a stand-alone—what we at the community college refer to as a "specialty" course (or, less generously, a "boutique" course). Might such a course, focusing as it does not on genocide but on the Shoah, attract enough students to run? Community college students, for reasons of expense and the need to balance commitments, are quite pragmatic in selecting their courses. Although our course does satisfy our college's general education requirement of a course with multicultural content, we could not be certain as to whether that would be a sufficient draw. In time, however, we learned never to underestimate the power of the Shoah to engage the imagination and commitment of our students. We built the course, and they came.

2 ▪ Discipline

Something as big as this catastrophe doesn't just happen without some sort of History giving evidence of what was to come.
Sharon, reading journal, February 2011

Reading this passage [from Ida Fink's short story "The Key Game"] helped me to stop thinking about the Shoah in broad strokes, and to start paying attention to the fine details.
Richard, reading journal, February 2011

Speaking for the Disciplines at a Community College

How do we know whether we are teaching effectively? How do we determine whether our students are learning what we want them to learn? All teachers understand that answering these questions will achieve positive outcomes. But how do we practitioners go about doing so? We concur with Lee Shulman that "teaching and learning . . . [are] domain-specific" rather than merely a product of generalized principles and strategies (Foreword vi). In other words, how we teach and how our students learn are questions necessarily tied to what comprises our course content. That content may include more than purely the facts (the formulas, key events, and concepts) of a subject but also the methods and ways of thinking characteristic of particular disciplines, what we refer to below as rhetorical processes. Furthermore, an assessment of teaching and learning should itself be grounded in those very research methodologies afforded by the disciplines. As advocates of Scholarship of Teaching and Learning rightly remind us, if research about teaching is to be seen as a scholarly project, then data must be subject to critique by peers and, if found worthy, distributed via publication for additional, scholarly exchange. This book represents our attempt at such research.

As faculty teaching at a public community college committed to general education, we might seem to be somewhat presumptuous in speaking for the disciplines—specifically, the disciplines of history and English studies (composition, rhetoric, and literary criticism)—as we do throughout this book. After all, the first two years of college aim to provide content knowledge of a discipline and not the rhetorical processes that get at how a historian or a critic thinks (Geisler 43). When our students take a class in British literature after 1918 or one in the history of the Civil War, they view such courses as subjects rather than disciplines (Nowacek 70). In other words, students in those courses expect to read with understanding the literature of that period or to learn the various causes and consequences of the Civil War. Gaining a knowledge of historiography or the use of textual evidence in history and literary criticism, for example, is not among the list of course outcomes—at least in a foundational or general education course. And yet, despite teaching at such an institution, we insist on speaking as disciplinary agents here.

Our rationale for doing so is both simple and complex: we are each a product of graduate study in particular disciplines, and were exposed to the rhetorical processes of those disciplines. Moreover, our course is aimed at honors students who have taken most of their general education courses and who are ready to confront significant challenges. Finally, the course is listed in the college's catalog as "Remembering the Holocaust in Literature and History: An Honors Interdisciplinary Seminar." Given that we put the word "disciplinary" right in our course title, we have a clear obligation to reveal explicitly what we mean by the terms "discipline" and "interdisciplinary." The latter term has been immensely difficult to define for our students (and, indeed, for ourselves), since we take it to mean integrating the disciplines of history, literature, and composition and rhetoric. What does true disciplinary integration mean, and how do we know when we see it? That is one of the key questions that we seek to address in this book.

Catching Glimpses of Disciplinary Understanding

Before we can address that question, we need to spell out for ourselves as well as for our students what it means to view the Shoah through the disciplinary lenses of history and English. The comments by Sharon and Richard that begin this chapter can help ground this discussion. Both students stopped what they were doing and took notice in new ways. In a weekly journal they were asked to identify a passage from a reading that seemed significant to them, describe their rationale for choosing that passage, and then reflect on how that passage broadened their understanding of the Shoah. Sharon responds to a work by the historian Rita Steinhardt Botwinick ("The Nazi Rise to Power"). Richard takes his cue from the short story writer Ida Fink ("The Key Game"). Even honors students struggle mightily with the metacognitively based question of how a reading broadens their understanding. Often students simply repeat their rationale for selection or ignore the question entirely in favor of summary. But here, in these brief statements, students begin to—as the composition scholar Ann E. Berthoff used to say—"think about thinking" (13). For her part, Sharon responds to a passage in which Botwinick draws a causal link between the rise of the Nazis and the national despair that gripped Germany following World War I. Sharon is prompted to bring up the subject of "History" (with a capital H). She observes that significant historical moments are the products of chronological and causal series of events. Sharon also notes—fleetingly—that such a chronology provided "evidence" for those alive at the time, who might have anticipated and forestalled the terrible outcome, and for those who come after the fact, who may use the chronology or causal chain for evidence in support of historical or critical interpretation. This insight, in which Sharon is not only looking *through* the window of history but also *at* the frame itself, is brief indeed, although she will go on to reveal that she had not realized how damaged Germany was between the wars. That realization, too, suggests a deeper form of learning than rehearsal of content.

No less complex or less fleeting, Richard's brief comment on the short story "The Key Game" offers evidence that he is beginning to acquire a critical, disciplinary perspective. Fink's story poignantly recounts one family's doomed attempt to survive the inevitable knock on the door and the sure deportation to come. A child is given a special responsibility—it is a "game"—to pretend that he is looking for a key before opening the door so as to give his father, who is being hunted, time to hide. The very fact that Richard calls attention to the act of reading as producing a change in his thinking is rare enough. Rarer is the realization that, prior to reading the story, Richard considered the Shoah's "broad strokes" only. We assume he means that before this moment his understanding of the Shoah could be summed up in the number, six million (the number of Jews exterminated) or in the names of the larger-than-life figures of the time—Hitler, FDR, Churchill, and Stalin, for example. But reading a short story compels Richard to pay attention to "finer details" of the Shoah. A bit later he references the "individual struggles" of those caught up in the Shoah (Richard 22 February 2011). Although Richard does not explicitly discuss the features of the short story as genre specific, he does, again fleetingly, point directly to the capacity of the writer to particularize and individualize human experience—the essence of literature. Paradoxically, Fink manages to ground the suffering of many by depicting the suffering of one family. Richard goes on to theorize based on his reading of the story: "Children were forced to mature years before any child should have to" (Richard 22 February 2011). Even as it particularizes, literature can provide useful, universal themes. Whether students are adept at extrapolating and reading for those themes is another matter. Richard seems poised to do so.

Paying Attention to Our Own Disciplinary and Pedagogical Differences

Creating the conditions for students to see the frame, as it were, and not simply gaze through the window of a discipline requires that instructors themselves stop to pay attention to their own disciplinary frames. How does a critic examine a text? How does a historian construe and construct the past? What constitutes a rhetorical analysis? All of us would do well to ask what ways of knowing distinguish our disciplines—whether they be physics, chemistry, sociology, or biology. If our own experience is a guide, doing so is challenging indeed. But here we have an advantage: we team-teach our course. We routinely come up against the strangeness of each other's discipline and need to articulate to the other the values and ways of knowing particular to our own fields.

When designing the course syllabus, for example, should we follow a strict chronological order? Should we, in other words, spend time on the events preceding the Shoah? Or should we descend immediately into the abyss? "Chronology matters," Ron often observes—especially to the work of the historian. Chronology and causation provide the foundation for historical analysis. Rita Steinhardt Botwinick offers a glimpse of the historian's approach:

> An understanding of the Holocaust *necessitates a comprehension* of the theory and practice of the Nazi movement. However, *before discussing what it meant to be a German* during the Third Reich, *we must consider the circumstances* which allowed Hitler to take control. . . . The government which *preceded* that of the Nazi Party was called the Weimar Republic. (64, 65; italics ours)

Historical events have causes—often multiple causes—and must be analyzed and understood, Botwinick implies. Chronology must be respected. Analysis and recollection of the past must be delivered logically and fluently.

While the New Historicism, with its attention to the historical context producing a work of literature, has had a generous impact on English studies, literary and rhetorical analysis of a text operate from a generally different set of assumptions and conventions from those of history. Genre, for example, may drive a critic's response. In other words, the special characteristics of a memoir or of a poem may elicit a response that has little to do with chronology or causation, the historian's tools. A memoir may be ordered less by external chronology and more by the associative logic of emotion and memory, a fact that Art Spiegelman makes abundantly clear in his attempt to bring his father's account of the war to the public in *Maus*. Try as Artie (the figure in the novel) might to get Vladek, his father, to be clear about the past, Vladek will tell his story in his way. A rhetorical analysis of a text might focus on Art Spiegelman's purpose in presenting Vladek's story in this way: to foreground the power of the individual mind to order the past as it sees fit or, as Spiegelman notes in an interview, to displace the "modernist cliché" of rendering the past in sequential order with a postmodern displacement of such order (Spiegelman, "Making").

Rhetorical and critical analysis alike will often pay attention to language, both in its figurative and literal expression. Spiegelman's symbolic use of a road in the shape of a swastika in one panel, for example, rivets the reader's attention. "Anja and I didn't have where to go," notes Vladek (*Maus I* 125). One of our students, Stefane, rightly comments in this way about the use of the symbol in the panel: "[T]he road that Vladek and Anja take is in the shape of a swastika[;] it's nearly foreshadowing in which I already know from the reading that the future of the couple would be one that will ultimately encounter the Nazis" (reading journal, April 2011). Stefane goes on to identify the pathos and typographical formation in the words at the bottom of the panel: "[A]nother aspect in analyzing this panel that jumps out is the words, they portray the feeling of desperation since the words 'WHERE TO GO?!' are capitalized [made bold], a question mark and exclamation is used at the end." Like the responses by Sharon and Richard, Stefane's analysis is not sustained; nevertheless, we are pleased to acknowledge their emerging disciplinary perspective.

Struggling to Integrate

Despite training in our particular disciplines, we must concur with the assessment of many who have studied and taught the Shoah: the usual certainties and conventions are liable to be overturned by this most complex and traumatizing subject. Indeed, as Lawrence Langer observes, Shoah literature has become its own genre, ripped free from the moorings of tradition ("On Writing" 4). Poems are written as fragments; diaries, composed at moments of terrible trauma and loss, come to us in a breathless frenzy. The idea of coolly and calmly recounting the event, as disciplined academicians might want, seems as absurd as offering reparations to the victims:

> Everything will be returned to its place,
> paragraph after paragraph.
> The scream back into the throat.
> The gold teeth back to the gums. (Pagis 4–7)

The poet's words, as we teach "Remembering the Holocaust in Literature and History," remind us not to stay confined within our own tidy, disciplinary rooms, but to be prepared to field questions without clear-cut answers and to move beyond the comfortable environs of our own academic specialties. Even as we strive to make explicit the varied tools of disciplinary analysis, we must acknowledge the limitations of those same tools.

Students over the years have given us plenty of evidence that the Shoah as a teaching subject typically disrupts rather than invites coherence; it so often provides evidence of disintegration rather than of integration. Students have reported having nightmares about the readings and have dropped the course as a result. At times students have stopped reading because the details were simply too graphic and dispiriting. One student, about whom Howard has written, simply stopped writing her weekly journal altogether, suffering, by her own account, significant writer's block (Tinberg). Later she would come to understand (and reveal through her culminating research project) the reason for that block: reading of the trauma suffered by Shoah victims was bringing to mind abuse that she suffered during an earlier period of her life. For her the affective response to suffering preempted and prevented a critical response—rendering silence preferable.

The journey toward integrated learning has not been an easy one, for us or for our students. It is safe to say that early on we stayed in our own rooms, metaphorically speaking (we have always been present in class as co-teachers). Our pedagogical approaches differed sharply. Understanding that students in this introductory course on the Shoah would require some kind of historical context, Ron favored the lecture approach, asking questions about historical events as given in the week's reading. His preferred mode was narrative: telling the story of the past. Less bound by chronology, Howard favored collaborative work, with students reading specific texts closely and working in small groups as they moved through a series of layered questions about those texts. The pedagogical differences early in the development of the course seemed stark indeed.

Disciplinary differences made themselves evident in the organization of the course as well. Each week our syllabus contained one reading from a conventional history and another from our anthology of literature. The first half of each class would be spent discussing the history and, after a break, the second half treated literature. We often recount, with some amusement now (less so then), the story of a small group of students who were enrolled as history majors at the university down the road. These students were intent on seeing our class as history (presumably to satisfy their major) and would leave each class at the break (we met then, as now, only once a week), as we shifted from history to literature. We suspect that these students remained convinced that this was indeed a history course. We aided and abetted in their misunderstanding, of course, by keeping the wall between our disciplines so firm. We have also encountered students who expected a course about literature, only to be disappointed that so much history was being discussed and read.

No doubt our decision to spend the first few weeks of the course providing important historical context contributed: the centuries-long history of antisemitism, the migration of the Jews to Eastern Europe, the seismic shock of World War I, the damaging retribution paid through the Treaty of Versailles, the onset of the Great Depression, and the rise of the National Socialist Party. We needed to put everything back into its place, "paragraph after paragraph," before proceeding to the Shoah itself. But was there another way to organize this course? Might we have aimed for a true integration of our disciplines? If so, how? And what might that integration have looked like? Is interdisciplinarity the same thing as integration? Or are the traditional methods and modes of inquiry associated with particular disciplinary domains blurred beyond recognition when fields cross? We were intent to go beyond, in Mary Huber and Sherwyn Morreale's apt phrase, "parallel play" (20). But in doing so we did not want to jettison for ourselves and for our students the useful lens afforded by traditional disciplines.

We are not certain that we accurately gauged the risks for our students if we transcended our appointed, disciplinary roles. Rebecca Nowacek tells this story about an interdisciplinary seminar that didn't go quite as planned:

> [T]wo instructors [break] their usual patterns of relatively limited interaction. The instructors identified this exchange as a moment of positive interdisciplinary interaction. The students,

however, expressed frustration bordering on anger about this same moment. Why? Because the instructors were breaking out of their usual patterns of instruction, out of their usual identity and roles. The shift was difficult and, in the students' eyes, inappropriate. (29)

We know that students come to our course with varied expectations—some expecting a full-fledged survey of literature from the Shoah and, as we have seen, some expecting a straight history course. But we can safely say that each student has expected a single instructor teaching from a singular vision. While we greatly appreciate a comment such as this (from a survey of our most recent course): "I've never taken an interdisciplinary class before and it definitely offers a unique (and in my opinion superior,) understanding of the material," we also take to heart the remark of one of our brightest students, who noted that he had taken the time to memorize as many facts and dates as he could for the midterm and noted with dismay that the exam called for little of that work. For this student, history, as he understood the term, needed to be more present in the form of facts to be learned and deployed.

Coming to Terms

As our course has evolved, we began to aim higher—specifically, to create the conditions for integrated learning. Since our entire project is designed to produce evidence of such learning, we think it prudent to spend time defining the term. We begin with this definition, produced by the Association of American Colleges and Universities, of "integrated thinkers":

> [I]ntegrative thinkers . . . can see connections in seemingly disparate information and draw on a wide range of knowledge to make decisions. They adapt the skills learned in one situation to problems encountered in another: in a classroom, the workplace, their communities, or their personal lives. (Association of American Colleges and Universities)

Such learning, then, is both transferable and intentional: in other words, integrative thinkers become, in Nowacek's terms, "agents of integration," making connections among disparate pieces of data and revealing a high level of awareness that they are doing so. Clearly integrated learning relies upon a sure understanding of disciplinary conventions and methods, even as it creates connections or common ground among disciplines. Moreover, although integrated learning represents a "cognitive advancement," it has an intense affective domain as well (Mansilla and Duraising 219; Nowacek 27). Students' excitement about learning motivates them to make such connections. Indeed, we surmise that integrated learning establishes connections not only between texts but between the affective and cognitive response to texts. The latter synthesis is especially noteworthy in a course about the Shoah, in which trauma is foregrounded.

We see such a synthesis forming in a reading journal composed by Micah, whose work seems especially integrative. In one journal, he is struck by this passage from Ida Fink's "A Spring Morning," a short story about a family—a mother, father, and their five-year-old child—awaiting inevitable arrest, deportation, and death:

> "Hush, darling," the woman answered, "lie still, as still as can
> be, like a mouse."
> "So they won't hear?"
> "So they won't hear."
> "If they hear us, they'll kill us," said the child. (246)

Finding the story "emotionally taxing to read," Micah does not do as others have done—simply turn away from the reading or shut off his critical response. He quickly notes the dissonance implied in the child's response, which "is a matter-of-fact declaration." "The child's understanding," he continues, "as well as her lack of emotion and seeming resignation, struck me."

He goes on to position this passage next to another in the story:

> When Mela says to Aron, "If we had known. . . . we wouldn't
> have had her. . . . She'll forgive us, Aron, won't she?" I felt that
> I got a better understanding of the incredible psychological toll
> that this calamity have wrought people (Fink 245).
> For a mother to have to question whether her child will for-
> give her for having brought her into a miserable world is such an

absurd sentiment that I could not help but feel vehement indigna-
tion as I read it. (Reading journal, February 2011)

Able to match his intense emotion with the critical assessment as to
the "psychological toll" expressed in these passages, Micah manages
to bridge an affective and cognitive response. But he goes even further
to consider the relationship between genre—specifically, the fictional
nature of Fink's work—and the emotional power expressed: "This
exchange, although between two ostensibly fictional characters, is one
of the most vivid and poignant scenes we have read thus far." Creating
the expectation that fiction would be less likely to convey authentic
truths than reporting of actual events, Micah asserts the contrary: that
fiction can convey a poignancy and power.

But it is his next move that is truly striking: Micah turns to
Abraham Lewin's "Diary of the Great Deportation," in which Lewin
offers firsthand reporting of the destruction and misery during the
Warsaw Ghetto's emptying by the Nazis. He locates this passage in the
diary: "Someone saves his sister and a four-year-old child, passing her
off as his wife. The child does not give the secret away. He cries out,
'Daddy!'" (Lewin 163). And he reflects on it thus:

> Again, this shows that such young children had at least a periph-
> ery understanding of what was happening, and they were cog-
> nizant enough to work toward self-preservation. These Jewish
> kids had to be attuned to what was happening. (Micah, reading
> journal, February 2011)

The children in the short story and in the diary become linked, in
Micah's mind. To move so skillfully between two different kinds
of text—a "work of imagination" and a work of witnessing—and to
establish a significant thread between them says much about Micah's
connection-making ability.

Micah's integrative habits of mind are also exhibited elsewhere
in his reflection upon the essay "Deniers, Relativists, and Pseudo-
Scholarship," in which Deborah Lipstadt argues that relativism merely
opens the door for deniers of the Shoah—and does so under the banner
of academic freedom. It is worth noting that in all the years of teaching the course, we had not included the subject of Shoah denial until

Spring 2011. We had not in part because we felt that the subject would invite an undisciplined and uncritical response, taking the form of the question How can people deny what is so obviously fact? We also worried that some students might be intrigued by a denier's argument or simply accept the view that everyone has a right to their own opinion. Still, given the possibility that our students might well encounter—if not a denial of the Shoah—a questioning of witness testimony, we thought it appropriate to bring up denial but in a scholarly and somewhat critical context, which Lipstadt provides.

Micah selects the following passage from Lipstadt's essay for his commentary:

> It is this commitment to free inquiry and the power of mythical thinking that explains, at least in part, how revisionists have attracted leading figures and institutions. Noam Chomsky is probably the best known among them. Chomsky wrote the introduction to a book by French revisionist Robert Faurisson. In it Chomsky argued that scholars' ideas cannot be censored no matter how distasteful they may be. (507)

We note, first of all, that Micah chooses not to focus on denial or deniers but rather on the academic matter of free and open discourse and the disciplinary challenge posed by revising history. He evokes the "idea of history" as "shaped by point of view" and "important to historical dialogue." Thus he takes issue with Lipstadt's view that revisionism is a kind of "mythical thinking." After all, he asserts, we would have little reason to question conventional accounts of the so-called discovery of the Americas if not for revisionist history. But while reserving the historian's right to revisit settled narratives about the past, Micah avows that "Holocaust denial is not another 'point of view' of the Holocaust." "There is no argument," Micah asserts: "The Holocaust happened." That last statement is less noteworthy, in our judgment, than the fact that Micah is able to achieve some awareness of what historians do or should do. In order to move back and forth among disciplines— occupying what Peter Galison (803) refers to as a "trading zone" among disciplines—Micah must also have an awareness of disciplinary ways of thinking. He seems well on his way toward acquiring that awareness.

Building a Model of Integrated Teaching and Learning for a Fragmented Subject

We are encouraged by responses such as Micah's, Richard's, Stefane's and Sharon's, as we have attempted, over the years, to construct a truly integrated model of teaching and learning. With most subjects, this would be a tall order, as disciplinary and institutional boundaries often seem impermeable and fixed. Even within English studies, for example, literary criticism and rhetoric too often have little to do with one another, despite the fact that collaboration makes so much sense: a critique of a poem, aside from a consideration of technical elements associated with the making of poetry, would benefit from an examination of a poem's rhetorical qualities—from the use of classical structures (such as synecdoche) to the poet's use of pathos.

Furthermore, we recognize the especially formidable challenge of integrating perspectives in a course on the Shoah, a subject that, as one scholar (among many) notes, is marked by disruption and loss:

> During the *Shoah,* an entire universe was shattered and dispersed in myriad directions. The remaining scattered fragments vary infinitely in size, shape and texture—from documents to diaries, testimonies to artifacts, photographs to works of art. Despite their wide dispersion, they can still be found in many places— government and private archives, libraries, and even in the attics and cellars of families who went through the vortex of the *Shoah.* (Rozett n. pag.)

A subject whose central feature is trauma by definition invites disrupted and fragmentary responses. Students may stop reading (and writing) when confronted with scenes of atrocity. Poets and artists, such as Dan Pagis and Samuel Bak, respectively, produce shards of verse or ruins of alphabetic text, as if acknowledging the inevitable lack of closure when one examines the Shoah. From an academic perspective, the act of disciplining inquiry becomes all too tempting: let us resort to the tools and methods that each of us knows best, goes the thinking—after all, they worked in the past.

We have come to know better: a subject as complex as the Shoah requires a complex and integrative approach. For example, we hope that our course produces an integration of the cognitive and affective domains. More specifically, we aim not only to allow some space for students to express their emotions when reading about trauma but also to encourage reflection as to the nature and causes and meaning of those emotions. Richard provides an interesting case study in that regard. He reads and responds to this troubling passage from Aharon Appelfeld's novel *Tzili*:

> And in the meantime the peasant woman beat [Tzili] constantly. She was old but strong, and she beat Tzili religiously. Not in anger but in righteousness. Ever since her discovery that Tzili was pregnant her blows had grown more violent, as if she wanted to tear the embryo from her belly. (314)

We would expect students to recoil from reading such a passage and then to express feelings of disgust and revulsion and leave it at that. But in asking the question, as we do in the weekly reading journal, "Why did you choose that passage?" we are encouraging a more thoughtful and integrated response. Richard lays out his readiness clearly when he writes, "After reading this passage, I felt compelled to analyze each character in order to better understand why I was affected by the passage" (reading journal, March 2011). While Richard does not explicitly state what feelings this passion aroused in him, we infer such an intense response that he has to dig deeper toward understanding. It is as if he feels a moral and critical imperative to do so. As he develops his thinking, Richard points out a parallel between the Nazis' treatment of women and children in the camps and the motives of the old woman (and others who mistreat Tzili) in the novel: In fact, he refers to the village women in the novel as "representations of concentration camp guards." Richard was likely thinking of various moments in our previous readings when women and children were singled out for brutal extermination by the Nazis. As Abraham Lewin notes in his diary about the liquidation of the Warsaw Ghetto, "It looks like there is a policy to liquidate women and children" (175). The Nazi war against Jewish women is being reenacted by these non-Nazi civilians, showing the extent of antisemitism at the time. This realization, together with the view that not only those Jews in camps and ghettos were treated brutally (Tzili survives the war in the forest), represents an important stage in Richard's "unlearning" and "relearning" process (Langer, "On Writing" 6).

Richard and other students are not alone in facing the challenge to rethink old knowledge. We, too, have had to unlearn and relearn as instructors. Pedagogically, we have come to see the limitations inherent in our own pedagogical approaches and come to see the virtues of an integrated or hybrid mode of teaching and learning. Howard's training in literary studies and in composition (including writing center work) have predisposed him to see students as "self-authoring"— generating an individualized, close reading of a text, for example—and as part of an interpretive community of peers. Hence he favors interactive discussions and collaborative work. In contrast, Ron's background in historical studies has led him to see students as receptors of key historical data and the instructor as generator of that data. Lecturing becomes an efficient mechanism of delivery. Each of us, however, has come to see the need to keep all these modes in play and, in fact, to synthesize these approaches. All of us—faculty and students—become authors in this model. Yet before authoring can properly occur, each of us needs to understand something of our prior knowledge.

3 ▪ What We Knew and When We Knew It

"I have taken many history courses but not enough to understand the Holocaust."

"I watched a movie about the Holocaust and I am excited about learning more about it."
Class transcript, January 2011

What Do We Bring?

After ten years as instructors we have learned that while we have increased our knowledge of the Shoah, we have mostly raised questions that lack definitive answers. Of course we know the facts and we can discuss the events, both long term and short, that led up to the Shoah and facts about the Shoah itself. "Few subjects have received as much rigorous scholarly attention as the Holocaust," writes historian Dan Porat (217). This point is reiterated by University of Chicago historian Bernard Wasserstein, who, in a recently published work on Jews in Europe prior to the Shoah, states,

> There exists a huge literature on the genocide of the Jews under Nazi rule. We know in precise detail almost every stage of the process by which the Nazis annihilated the Jews in every country of occupied Europe. (xxi)

We can even discuss some of the controversies among Shoah historians, such as those between the intentionalists and the functionalists—those who believe that the Shoah was predetermined by the Nazi regime and those who believe that it developed more incrementally. From a literary perspective we can also explicate the stories, poems, and memoirs that we assign and discuss the problem.

While we remain convinced that this is an important course for our students to take, we continue to struggle with how to answer those fundamental but crucial questions we know will eventually be raised: for example, How could something as horrific as the Shoah have been allowed to happen? Or, as Eva Hoffman asks, "What meaning does the Holocaust hold for us today?" (ix). In trying to deal with such fundamental but crucial questions we want to help our students also to be able to deal with "man's repeated inhumanity to man" (Porat 218).

Such matters are on our minds as we begin a new semester of teaching this course. Although there is always a feeling of excitement and anticipation that we bring to each new class, we also bring a feeling of angst and dread. Teaching the subject of the Shoah drains us. We know that there are no sure answers to the questions that we will raise and there is no easy way to proceed. We are in agreement with Lindquist that "one does not teach the Holocaust as much as one confronts it" (21). Nevertheless, we believe that despite our own doubts and the emotional toll that we ourselves experience, the course needs to be taught. It is important at the very least that students learn as much about the facts as possible and be able to counter those who would deny or trivialize the Shoah. We do hope that at least some of the students will learn even deeper lessons from their study of the Shoah, and we hope that the way we have constructed the course will help facilitate that process.

We know that, as with any subject, students need to build on prior knowledge in order to come to an understanding of the course material. Based on our initial introduction to the students in this class, we determine a high interest in the subject, but little knowledge. However, our goals remain ambitious. In the first class we explain how we came to teach the course and our reasons for continuing to do so over the past seven years. We make no bones about the fact that we know the course will be challenging on both the cognitive and affective levels. In class discussions and in their weekly writing assignments we expect them to be both fully engaged with the subject but also able to stand back and be critical, to accept that there might not be answers to some of their questions. We also indicate that much of what they would be reading, seeing, and hearing from survivor testimonies will be difficult to deal with and perhaps even to accept. We acknowledge that there are those who would deny the Shoah or at least diminish its importance and we want these students to be armed with the facts and be able to refute such accusations. We hope that through the way we constructed the course and our willingness to be as open as possible we will be able to help them to navigate this very difficult terrain.

What Do Our Students Bring?

Despite the questions and reservations, we still look forward to introducing the Shoah to a new group of honors students. After going over preliminaries such as introducing the texts, discussing the various assignments, and describing the grading system, we pose these questions: What do the students bring to this study? What is their prior knowledge of the subject, and from what source or sources did they obtain it? Are students prepared to deal with what they are going to encounter? This process provides us and the class with a starting point. We go around the room and ask each student what they know about the Holocaust and where they learned it.

Students' experiences vary, while tending to be superficial. Some students have been introduced to the Shoah by reading the *Diary of Anne Frank,* a text many students read in middle or high school. One reports that "ever since I read the book, I have been interested in learning more about it" (class transcript, January 2011). Another student in the same class wants to go "beyond what happened in that attic." He wants a better understanding of the Holocaust and to figure out what role religion played. Why, he wonders, did it happen to the Jewish people? This is a fundamental question for many of our students, since most have had little contact with Jewish people and even less exposure to Judaism. Consequently, we spend a brief time at the start of the class reviewing Jewish history.

Other students' interest in the Shoah is stimulated by movies that provide an introduction to its horror, particularly *Schindler's List.*

Although such films may be important, they lack the explanatory material that would help viewers understand the subject in any depth, and in some cases can even be misleading. However, as one of our students, Stefane, says in our discussion, watching *Schindler's List* made her want to learn more. Richard had watched the more recent movie *Life is Beautiful,* but he also felt that he needed context to understand what was going on, that he lacked detailed knowledge, and that movies that emphasize violence "desensitize" people.

For other students it is an interest in history as a subject that draws them to the course. Mariah felt that the absence of any real discussion about the Shoah in history classes "was disappointing" and she wanted to learn more about it as a way of expanding her understanding of that historical period (class transcript, January 2011). We know that the Shoah generally receives only a cursory treatment in many school and college history surveys. This omission is reinforced by Richard's statement that, although he had taken a number of history courses, he had learned very little about the Shoah and felt he should know more (class transcript, January 2011). Peter also has an interest in World War II because his grandfather had died in a Japanese POW camp, a fact that motivates him to want to learn more about the Shoah (class transcript, January 2011). At the same time, Micah and Sharon are interested in literature and are drawn to the course in part to learn more about the Shoah from that perspective (class transcript, January 2011). One student even took the course primarily because he likes the teaching style of one of the instructors, although he said he also felt it was important to learn about "the darker side of life" (class transcript, January 2011).

Few students have a personal connection to the Shoah itself. Stacey's grandmother was a Holocaust survivor, but Stacey knows little about what happened to her; being Jewish she felt that she should know more (class transcript, January 2011). Andreea, a first-generation immigrant from Romania, tells the class that her grandmother was caught up in the Holocaust but survived, although she lost most of her family. It is not clear from her initial statement whether her grandmother or her lost family members were Jewish. Still Andreea wants to learn about the events that her family had been caught up in (class transcript, January 2011). Michael's grandfather was a medic during World War

II and helped to liberate one of the camps. He had not received much information from his grandfather and hopes the course will help him learn more about what had occurred (class transcript, January 2011).

Constructing a Course

We have already described something of the nature of this course as it has developed over time. Lindquist quotes the axioms that "you can't teach what you don't know" and "you can't teach what you don't know how to teach" (22). We appreciated from the inception of the course that we had much to learn in terms of content as well as the pedagogical challenges in teaching such an explosive subject. Nevertheless, we thought it important that we start teaching the course and learn as we go. We went through a number of changes through the years. One of those areas of change had to do with the choice of a history text.

For a number of years, we used a survey history text on the Shoah by Rita Steinhardt Botwinick that is organized both chronologically and thematically (*History*). Since most of our students come into the course with very little background information on the history of the period and certainly on the Shoah, we thought that this text could provide them with the basic facts they would need. Botwinick was a member of the Kindertransport, in which approximately ten thousand children were sent to England to stay with British families. She was one of the few who actually were reunited with their parents (Botwinick, *History* 10). As a professor of history and a survivor of the Shoah, she attempts to balance a historian's objectivity with her own personal story. There is clearly a question of whether such objectivity is even possible, especially with a subject as emotionally laden as the Shoah, yet there is the expectation that a historian will retain that stance. Some of our students even commented that they thought Botwinick had inserted herself too often into the text. Although this provided a good opportunity to discuss the possible limits of objectivity, after a few years of teaching the course we decided to try another approach.

Since an important objective of the course was to help our students develop the ability to look critically at sources as well as gain knowledge about the facts of the Shoah, we assigned two different types of historical texts: David Engel's *The Holocaust: The Third Reich and the Jews* and Donald Niewyk's *The Holocaust: Problems and Perspectives in Interpretation*. We chose the former text because it treated the facts of the Shoah in a compact form, and presented key documents in the second part of the book. We saw the Niewyk text offered an opportunity for students to gain an understanding of some of the controversies surrounding Shoah scholarship, including the nature of resistance and the possibility of rescue. Each chapter features three to four different historians or social scientists who take different positions on these topics. In his introduction, Niewyk argues,

> Historical and scientific information is useless until someone tries to make sense of what is happening—tries to explain why and how things developed the way they did. In making these analyses and conclusions, however, both historians and scientists often come to disagree vehemently about the underlying reasons for what they have observed or discovered and sometimes about the observations themselves. (xv)

This is a key point: scholars can disagree on fundamental facts. Too often, students receive a very different message, notably from textbooks: that unanimity of opinion among historians exists routinely. We tasked ourselves to construct a course that would accomplish a great deal in fifteen weeks. If we were teaching the course only from an historical perspective and we wanted them just to learn the facts of the Shoah, that goal might be accomplished. However, we were more ambitious; three other texts helped us to move toward a more comprehensive understanding of the subject.

For the literary portion of our course, we initially chose Albert H. Friedlander's *Out of the Whirlwind: A Reader of Holocaust Literature*. Although this text introduced students to particular writers and theologians' takes on aspects of the Shoah, it lacked a critical apparatus that placed the works in a meaningful context. We then discovered a more comprehensive and scholarly collection of Shoah literature, *Out of the Ashes: A Holocaust Anthology*, by the preeminent Shoah scholar Lawrence Langer. This text has exposed students to the range of Shoah literature—including memoirs, poems, short stories, and even a short novel by Aharon Appelfeld. Of course, given time limits we can expose students only to a sampling of the voluminous literature in this area.

Since our overall goal is to expose students as much as we are able to the who, why, and what of the Shoah, we also felt the need to introduce them to two issues that would complicate their understanding of the subject. One is reflected in the work of Princeton political scientist Jan Gross, who, in *Neighbors,* makes it clear that the killers of the Shoah were not necessarily Germans or Nazis. In this controversial work, Gross describes how the non-Jewish inhabitants of a small Polish town turned on their Jewish neighbors and, in one terrible day, murdered most of them. This work also attempts to illustrate how the crime was hidden from the outside world for many years—until it was revealed in a single document discovered by the persistent Gross. Since this is such an important and startling work, we have assigned it from the inception of the course. Because it is both a work of history and historiography (not only relating the events of the past but also how that record was created), *Neighbors* began to steer us toward a consideration of how the Shoah has been represented.

The last work that we chose, and have used from the inception of the course, is *Maus,* by Pulitzer Prize winner, graphic artist, storyteller, and child of survivors Art Spiegelman. This wonderful work is so powerful that we felt that it had to be included. Spiegelman tells the story of his father's and mother's travails from pre-Shoah days through the Shoah and beyond. Just as in *Neighbors,* which attempts to tell the larger story of the Shoah from the perspective of a single village, in *Maus* students are provided a micro view of one's family's experience while they gain insights into the larger world of the Shoah. Spiegelman's method of interviewing his father over a period of time and relating his story in comic form—with Jews portrayed as mice, Germans as cats—is, of course, startling to students, but at the same time very effective (see chapter 2 for a discussion of Spiegelman's work). Students often take to the book and have read it before we actually discuss it toward the end of the course. As Richard notes,

> *Maus* puts it all together. Although it is one person's tale, we can relate to what we have read and discussed and we get the big picture. . . . [I]t felt like you were in a movie the whole time and

the symbolic use of "cat" and "mouse" helped. (Reading journal, April 2011)

A key figure in *Maus* is, of course, Vladek, Art Spiegelman's father. Some students are put off by Vladek, who often comes across in the text as overbearing. Nevertheless, they admire his ability to survive under such horrific conditions. Richard, in fact, relates to the situation of father and son since his parents are immigrants, and he can connect Vladek's diction and actions to those of his own father (reading journal, April 2011).

We remain satisfied with the way that the Langer, Gross, and Spiegelman texts aid in achieving our course objectives, but we are less satisfied with the history texts. Although we want the students to learn the facts of the Shoah, we are particularly interested in examining issues related to historiography and various controversies present in Shoah studies. In our eighth year of teaching the course, we settled on *The Holocaust: Readings and Interpretations*. This work, edited by community college instructors Joseph and Helen Mitchell, treats the subject comprehensively and features articles by noted scholars such as historian Yehuda Bauer and sociologist Nechama Tek, both of whom comment on resistance, and former Catholic priest and journalist James Carroll, who discusses the role of the Catholic Church during the Shoah. We decided to continue with our chronological approach in the first part of the course and then shift to a more topical direction, addressing such issues as gender and history and memory. The Mitchell and Mitchell text, along with the others we assign, allowed us to do both.

We are also cognizant of the importance of employing pedagogy that we hope will fulfill, or at least approximate, our aims. The Shoah scholar Michael Bernard-Donals asks what he calls a "simple question": "What do teachers and students hope to accomplish when speaking, teaching and writing about the Shoah?" (263). He wonders how the Shoah can be represented in a way that is compelling and understandable. We hope to do so, but, as Bernard-Donals observes, "conventional accounts of learning may fail, particularly when it comes to the Holocaust" (264). We have recognized this to be true—hence we have struggled in our choice of texts.

But, of course, printed texts are not sufficient in and of themselves. We realize that employing multimedia can be important. Drawing on the rich archive of survivor testimony from the United States Memorial Holocaust Museum and the University of Southern California Shoah Foundation, we utilize excerpts of survivor testimony as related to the topic at hand for each class. We also began each class with authentic music from the period, usually a song sung in Yiddish or German. In addition, each year, including our eighth year, we have invited speakers, most of whom are survivors or the children of survivors. Their presentations are given about halfway through the semester, and prove to be very compelling.

We have been clear that this is not a lecture class per se. We have envisioned each class as a dialogue between students and students and between students and instructors. To facilitate this process, students submit journal entries consisting of three parts: a passage from the readings, the reason for choosing the passage, and an explanation of how it broadened the student's understanding of the Shoah. The purpose of the assignment is to facilitate a close reading of the texts as well as reflection and discussion of what they are reading. We spend the first part of the class having students read from their journals; for bonus points they can write in the following week's journal entry about what struck them as interesting or cogent about a classmate's reaction to a passage and why. Again, our purpose is to help students to develop or enhance their ability to be metacognitive. This ability is not always common in young adults, or even older students who have not had practice reflecting on what they read or hear. To go beyond learning the facts of a subject, to develop the ability to examine text critically, necessitates creating a structure and practice that enhance development. This is particularly true when dealing with a subject like the Shoah, which is so emotionally fraught and of which the students begin with only superficial knowledge.

The culmination of the course is a project that asks students to develop and research a significant question about the Shoah and to represent their findings as a web page or digital snapshot. This assignment calls upon students to employ a variety of modalities now available to them. Although this is clearly challenging for many of the students, they have been able, for the most part, to rise to the challenge and complete the assignment with impressive results. On the last day of class, the students are required not to summarize their results but to describe briefly the process they followed in constructing their work. We hope students gain an in-depth understanding of some aspect of the Shoah using the latest technologies as well as gain increased experience conducting research. As honors students who will—for the most part—transfer to a baccalaureate institution, they will need these skills.

Developmental Challenges

Although many of our students have derived a great deal from the course, we know that there are limits based not only on the survey-style nature of the course, but also on the developmental limitations of many of our students at this stage in their academic careers.

Important research in the last thirty years on cognitive and affective development in college students and beyond has given us a framework within which to discuss student development. Cognitive and developmental psychologists and educators such as Perry; Belenky, Field, Goldberger, and Tarule; Baxter-Magolda; and Kegan (Kegan, *Evolving; In Over*) have developed age and stage theories that help us map out how students might be looking at the world and what steps can be taken to foster their growth intellectually and emotionally. Building on earlier research by Piaget and Erikson, these researchers have demonstrated that development can be a lifelong endeavor. Perry and Belenky, Field, Goldberger, and Tarule have developed age and stage theories that help us better understand how college students can move from being concrete to abstract learners. Their theories demonstrate the trajectory a learner can follow as they are confronted with more complex material in their classes. This transition does not occur suddenly, but follows a more or less predictable path—making allowances, of course, for individual idiosyncrasies.

We are particularly influenced by Robert Kegan, who, working from a social constructionist framework, "attends to developments in an individual's very 'construction' of reality, how he or she makes meaning" (*In Over* 202). Kegan sees meaning systems as having the potential to change as individuals are challenged to go beyond the "system" in which they are embedded in order to develop the capacity to be "self-reflective" and "self-corrective" (*In Over* 225). In his five-stage model from infancy through adulthood, Kegan points to the challenges facing educators like ourselves who want students to go beyond concrete forms of learning and pat or simple answers to complex questions. Surely the Shoah calls upon such ways of knowing. When students come to us, they see the world dualistically and may very well view the Shoah as pitting good versus evil—not an unreasonable perspective. But they then encounter dissonance when, for example, they see Jewish policemen harming Jewish civilians in a ghetto. What new perspective must emerge in order for students to understand such a development?

Kegan and others suggest creating "the necessary scaffolding, or more aptly, the necessary bridge" that would allow for the movement from one form of understanding or meaning to another (*In Over* 43). One such instance, writes Kegan, is the difference between an example and a definition—if by the first we mean a "concrete" fact, and by the second we refer to "abstract generalization" (*In Over* 53). In our study of the Shoah it is important, for example, that students move from telling the story of the Holocaust to examining the impact of the form or genre of historical work on our understanding of it. In the remainder of this book we examine to what extent we have succeeded in assisting students in this transition by demonstrating how history is written so as to lay the groundwork for an even more complex consideration of the historian's sifting facts and making inferences (Gabb, Tinberg, and Weisberger 105).

4 ▪ Bystanders and Agents

Being a bystander, a passive witness, was perhaps a moral failing, even a moral crime.
Ellen Cassedy, We Are Here

The Bystander

What does it mean to be a bystander in the context of the Shoah? Were bystanders ordinary people who were neither perpetrators nor victims and who might have acted but did nothing (Niewyk 180)? During that period a great many people both in Europe and the United States did very little or looked the other way. This, of course, raises the question of culpability: Could more have been done to save the Jewish population, who were murdered wholesale by the Nazi regime? We explicitly raise this question in our class. We consider the role of the Vatican in failing to sufficiently help the Jewish population in Europe and regard the behavior of so-called indifferent accomplices, those who stood by as the Shoah proceeded (Carroll; Sterling 183–92). In this chapter we will examine the behavior of the bystander in the Shoah per se. But we hope also to use the bystander metaphorically, as a kind of lens through which to view our own role, as students and faculty, in studying the subject: What conditions promote an effective level of engagement, and what inhibits that engagement? In other words, are those of us who teach and study the Shoah destined to be only bystanders, or can we have greater agency as we confront the challenge of teaching and studying such a course?

Laying the Groundwork for Engagement

If our goal is to engage our students fully in this course, can we help them to get beyond being merely bystanders to the subject? As Bernard-Donals points out, we can learn the facts, but "[i]n the case of the Holocaust, what often drops out is the horror, or the why" (265). This disengagement is understandable, of course. Who wants to enter the gates of Auschwitz or relive life in the Warsaw or Lodz ghettoes? And yet, if our course is to have any chance of success, we have to make the effort to assist our students to go beyond being a mere bystander to this history.

We begin our course with a story entitled "The Spinoza of Market Street," by the great Yiddish writer and Nobel laureate Isaac Bashevis Singer. The story depicts an intellectual—a follower of the seventeenth-century philosopher Baruch Spinoza—one Fischelson, who lives in prewar Warsaw. He is down on his luck and lives above a major street in the city, which is inhabited by a range of individuals—including merchants, craftspeople, and day laborers.

Fischelson is a spectator. His bible, Spinoza's *Ethics,* and his prior experience have caused him to despise the material world and all those in it. Fischelson is an observer who, despite his erudition, has little understanding of the life he views from his perch above the street. However, his mind and body having deteriorated, and seemingly near death, Fischelson is rescued by a woman. Black Dobbe is a person quite his opposite, but who, as one of our students writes, helps him experience the "warmth" and "happiness" that "his mind has forbidden him" (Andreea, reading journal, February 2011).

Few students grasp the bystander theme. For example, Mariah is puzzled by Fischelson's ironic exclamation to his hero Spinoza at the end of the story, "[F]orgive me. I have become a fool." To her mind, Fischelson has succumbed to life's physical passions. In our roundtable discussion, she argued that he had betrayed his principles by marrying Dobbe. The idea that he, in fact, might have finally chosen to engage more fully in life and reject his bystander status is not reflected in her oral statement or her journal (Mariah, reading journal, February 2011). Other students similarly do not comment on Fischelson's bystander behavior. Robert, for example, chooses a passage that describes Jewish life in prewar Warsaw, but makes no mention of the character as bystander (reading journal, February 2011). Only Andreea comments on Fishelson as an outsider. She observes,

> [He] would rather isolate himself from such things and live a lonely, bleak life. It is evident that reading the passage, he is this way due to his past experiences. After meeting Dobbe, he has a completely different outlook on life. This tells me that being a loner is not the man he honestly is. His heart longs for "warmth" and "happiness," but his mind has forbidden him from forgetting the past. (Reading journal, February 2011)

However, when asked how the passage she chose enhances her understanding of the Shoah she fails to make the connection to the role of the bystander during the war.

The Lure of History: Remaining a Bystander

In our third class, readings deal with the ascension to power of the Nazi Party in Germany and the events leading up to the Nazi takeover in 1933. In one sense we hope that our students will acquire historical facts while being led deeper into the Shoah. Yet we remain concerned that students will assume the passive role of bystander to history, absorbing fact after fact without acting, or critically reflecting, upon what they have learned. Stefane references Elie Wiesel's charge to "the world's conscience to realize that you are/were a bystander during such evil; you could not escape guilt or shame" (reading journal, February 6, 2011). Although she picks up on the term "bystander," her explanation of how it broadens her understanding of the Shoah deals with such facts as the Treaty of Versailles and the downturn of the German economy after World War I, allowing her to understand the rise of the Nazi Party. Richard, for his part, focuses on looking for concrete historical causes for the Nazis rise to power. After all, he notes,

> The Treaty of Versailles embarrassed all Germans as a whole by blaming them for World War I. The German people needed

revival, to escape the shackles that the 1920s placed them in. Hitler and others like him knew this, and what better scapegoat to choose than the Jews? (Reading journal, February 2011)

A number of students are shocked by the fact that someone like Hitler, with his racist ideology, would be acceptable to the German people. One student takes from one week's reading on Nazi ideology that Germans hated Jews just as "today's Israelis . . . are hated by so many Arabs" and that "more often than not it is usually uneducated who simply don't know any better than to follow the crowd"(Peter, reading journal, February 2011). Stacey says she learned the following from the same reading:

> I never really understood how deep the Nazi hatred of Jews was.
> . . . The movies, and the history books address the Holocaust as one of a long series of events that resulted from Hitler's reign, and from the war itself. I now understand that it was the Nazi hatred of Jews that was the primary impetus for the cold blooded murder of six million. (Reading journal, February 2011)

In contrast, Michael jumps to this conclusion from the same reading: "It shows that Nazis were men, just as we are now. Desperate times try us all, and we must maintain our humanity and compassion for all, lest we end up justifying acts of barbarism in defense of nonsense ideology" (reading journal, February 2011). In bringing the discussion back to ourselves ("just as we are now"), Michael attempts to break out of the bystander position, despite the many temptations to accept the historical accounts of the time passively and dispassionately.

We see another student following Michael's lead. After reading the John Weiss's "The Ideology of Death," Andreea is shocked when she learns that the "Bishop of Linz wrote a pastoral letter about 'degenerate' Judaism in 1932" (reading journal, February 2011). She continues, "This passage captured my attention because as a devout Christian myself, I am truly offended by his message. . . . [H]ow could Christians of true faith hear this message and agree with it?" Her explanation is that the Germans were "brainwashed" by Hitler, which is "the only explanation I have for the letter" (reading journal, February 2011).

What do we make of these reactions? The students in their various ways try to come to terms with the fact of the Shoah. But this is just the beginning of the course and despite personal reactions of shock and dismay they remain bystanders to the events they are studying. Perhaps Stacey, the only Jewish student in the class, comes closest to reading the text in a more personal way when she writes that "my relatives, who witnessed the Holocaust first hand, never said much about it; I think they were trying to forget" (reading journal, February 2011). While she was one of the least forthcoming of the students in the class (and, perhaps for understandable reasons), it seems to hit home to her that being Jewish in Nazi-controlled Europe constituted a death warrant. As she notes,

> This puts my understanding of the Holocaust in a new light. War can be avoided through political discussion. Ideological differences can be resolved through negotiation. A Jew, however, is born a Jew, and whether he or she observes religious traditions or not, marries a Jew, or not, is buried as a Jew, or not . . . no political discussion can change the fact that a Jew is a Jew . . . , and for the Nazis nothing could temper the racial hatred that resulted in the Shoah. It happened because it had to. (Reading journal, February 2011)

At this early point in the semester students watched testimony, via a web archive, from a witness to Kristallnacht, the event that made it clear to the world what the fate of the Jews in Germany would be. Kurt Messerschmidt, who survived the Shoah, recounts the event: In 1938, as a young man, he and a friend had observed an old Jewish man being forced by two SA to pick up shards of glass, "one by one, while a crowd watched." Their reaction upon coming to this scene was to get off their bicycles and help the man pick up the glass. Whether those in the crowd approved or not, they were bystanders who did nothing but observe. The two took the only action they could, says Messerschmidt. We make the point that testimony, given years after the event, has considerable value in helping us to get beyond the sometime bare and cold facts of our texts. (We have more to say about the importance of testimony in the next chapter). More pertinent to our own concerns here, Messerschmidt's actions at the time highlight the difference in this case between being a bystander and a participant: What would have happened, Messerschmidt wonders, if others had joined in to assist the old man? This line of inquiry becomes more urgent as we move more deeply into the Shoah itself, and discuss a fictional story by Ida Fink and the memoir of life in the Warsaw Ghetto by Abraham Lewin.

Can We Remain Bystanders in the Ghetto?

We now discuss the events leading to the Shoah itself, beginning with the invasion of Poland by the Germans and the subsequent roundup of the Jewish population in large cities such as Warsaw or Krakow as well as smaller towns and villages. Students may hold such events at arm's length; keeping themselves at a proper distance. After all, these are facts which, while important, are merely facts nevertheless. To this point, the Shoah seems somewhat abstract.

Yet upon reading Abraham Lewin's "Diary of the Great Deportation," the historical debate gives way to the more intimate connection with what is happening on the ground. Samantha's journal entry reveals a degree of engagement, for example:

> Mr. Lewin's "Diary of the Great Deportation" . . . has set my mind wild creating new images of the Shoah. Through his first-hand account of what life was like for a great number of Jewish people, their plight has become something more real to me. The fact that the day was wonderfully beautiful, yet the "slaughterer [was] slaughtering" seems like a description of something surreal that Mr. Lewin (along with all of the other Jews) were having an incredibly hard time coming to terms with. . . . To be able to look at the sky and still see its wonder at a time like the Shoah was hard enough, especially when in the same breath Mr. Lewin saw the "slaughterer . . . slaughtering." (Reading journal, February 2011)

Like Samantha, Hillary begins to empathize with what was happening to Lewin and the events of the Shoah when she chooses one sentence to quote from Lewin's diary: "We are preparing ourselves for death. What will be our fate?" (161). She says she chose to write about the passage "because there are a lot of complexities within it." She goes on to explain,

It stuck with me while I read the rest of the journal. I felt it represented a lot. I also couldn't help but think how terrifying it must have been to have these thoughts. Abraham Lewin had to be a very stout hearted person to be able to face this terrifying fact to the point where he actually was able to write it down. (Reading journal, February 2011)

What she learns from reading the passage is particularly poignant when she connects the reading to the testimony we had heard from Kurt Messerschmitt the week before. She observes,

This journal was similar to the testimony we watched in class. It delivers a personal story with unique details. Being able to be immersed into someone's inner thoughts is extremely valuable. . . . [R]eading this journal made me realize just how frightened they must have been. This passage, in particular, made me think about life as a Jew during the Shoah. (Reading journal, February 2011)

Interestingly, Hillary then backs off to become more analytical, and reports, "I think it is safe to say that this passage didn't enlighten me as much as the journal in its entirety. However, it did spark interest which made me read on and research to try and find answers or explanations."

Hillary, of course, is rightly reacting to our desire for students both to immerse themselves in the material and to go beyond being a mere bystander to the events of the Shoah, but at the same time to read with a critical eye. Whether this is possible at this point in their intellectual development is a question we address in a subsequent chapter. Nevertheless, it is clear that by this point in the semester most of the students are engaged. This becomes clear in their reactions to not only the Lewin diary but to the other readings for the fourth class: two short stories by the great Shoah writer Ida Fink, "The Key Game" and "A Spring Morning."

Both stories feature children as victims of the Shoah—which, of course, resonates with our students. We have already mentioned Richard's reaction to "The Key Game," a story that encompasses the horror of the Shoah in miniature, with its focus on a family awaiting the dreaded knock on the door. In "A Spring Morning," a family has already been abducted by the SS and are being marched to their deaths.

The father, seeing a desperate glimmer of hope for his young daughter, sends the young child into a crowd of bystanders, only to have her shot in front of him. Picking up the dead child, he "waited for a second shot but all he heard was a shout and he understood that they would not kill him here, that he had to keep on walking, carrying his dead child" (Fink, "A Spring Morning" 248). Stefane responds this way:

> [I]t was very emotional to me. It really shows that the father's last attempt to save his daughter was pointless and that their lives were already carved in stone by the Germans to be discarded like animals. There is no way understanding how this could possibly [have] happened; there no way one can even read about this terrible story and not shed a tear. (Reading journal, February 2011)

At this point, Stefane, like many of the other students in the class, has begun to feel the impact of the Shoah in a visceral way.

Micah's reading of Fink's stories points to the way in which a fictionalized account can have great power and open the door for students to be emotionally engaged with the subject. He says,

> Fink's stories are the first in the class that I actually found emotionally taxing to read; as I read the previously assigned essays, I was shocked and disgusted to be sure, but somehow Fink's fabricated accounts resonated more profoundly with me. The way she captured the family dynamics that emerged during the Shoah, as well as the desperation and guilt of Jewish parents was effective and artful. (Reading journal, February 2011)

Micah reveals the emotional impact of what he is reading and at the same time appreciates the way Fink is able to convey in this fictionalized account some of the reality of the Shoah. In his journal for the week he connects also with Lewin's nonfiction memoir by focusing on its effect on children and families. He writes, "The inhumanity and perverseness shocked and pained me. Other essays we have read spoke to this. . . . However, it was not until I read these pieces that the human aspect of this revealed itself and that I began to get a sense of just how nightmarish and harrowing an environment it must have been." Jacob concurs with Micah: the "human aspect" is hard to ignore. Jacob observes,

Through our studies so far, the sufferings of the Shoah have certainly been hard to comprehend, yet this reading broadened my understanding through yet another dimension of the devastation. While the pain of mistreatment, abuse and even torture was abysmal, it was even more damaging to live with the fact that likely your loved ones will suffer such conditions. . . . [S]eeing your loved ones suffer in such unimaginable ways is perhaps the greatest agony a human could experience. (Reading journal, February 2011)

Standing By in the Camps

These works have a powerful effect on our students. However, we appreciate the limits to how far one can stray from a bystander position when studying the Shoah. Reflecting this truth, French filmmaker Claude Lanzmann observes that the Holocaust is "unique in that it erects a ring of fire around itself, a borderline that cannot be crossed because there is a certain ultimate degree of horror that cannot be transmitted" (quoted in Bernard-Donals 190). Lanzmann, of course, is director of what is arguably the best movie made on the Holocaust, *Shoah*. This film approaches the Shoah through a long series of harrowing interviews "with people who had been in the closest proximity or contact with those who were murdered as they went to their deaths" (Rieff 41). These people include guards, SS officials, and, most of all, survivors, some of whom were members of the "so-called *Sonderkommandos*, the special details whose task it was to lead the doomed to the gas chambers and dispose of their bodies after their murder" (Rieff 42). Hardly bystanders, the Sonderkommandos assume the peculiar and complex positions of both perpetrators (or agents) and victims, since most would themselves perish—a fact that poses special challenges for many of our students, for whom the Shoah pits good against evil, perpetrator against victim.

Although we don't screen *Shoah* itself, we can see in journal entries and class discussions that by the fourth week of class the readings and interviews with survivors have had their effect on students. They are beginning to go beyond a superficial knowledge of the subject and moving at least some distance from being merely a bystander in their studies. The readings in our fifth week push this process forward somewhat as we zero in on the experience of two prominent survivors, Primo Levi and Charlotte Delbo. The readings provide students with insights into the camps themselves as well as post-Shoah reactions from these two very perceptive and skillful writers.

A number of students react to Levi's discussion of the feeling of "shame," which some survivors carried with them after liberation. Many of our students are perplexed that Levi, for one, would ask forgiveness for being a bystander amid others' suffering, and so long after the fact. For Micah, the revelation is stunning. He notes,

> [Levi] is talking about resisting the Nazis, and explains that he feels he has to excuse himself for his inaction. That he still contemplates this idea so many years after the fact shows that many of these survivors never fully left the Shoah behind. (Reading journal, February 2011)

Stefane expresses her own puzzlement:

> It puzzles me in a way that I question why this man is trying to justify his actions. . . . This introduces me [to the idea] that life after the Shoah was a life always questioned by the individual. . . . a continuing tortuous life just as terrible as death. (Reading journal, February 2011)

Peter was just as perplexed at this outcome: "for Levi to feel haunted decades after seeing others suffer and knowing that he couldn't do anything . . . it made me stop and try to understand what he would feel guilty about that and I wasn't able to" (reading journal, February 2011). Of course we know that Levi eventually committed suicide, as did other survivors—something the students had a hard time understanding, since it does not fit in with the so-called happy ending scenario that they might have hoped for. Nor did Levi's harsh assessment of his own inaction jibe with students' somewhat dualistic view of bystanders and agents. This is a distance that they would not be able to traverse easily, if at all.

5 ▪ Witnesses

Above all, we need the witness. There is no Holocaust history without witnesses.
Yehuda Bauer, "Is the Holocaust Explicable?"

We must be capable of listening to lonely voices reaching us from the abyss.
Jan T. Gross, Neighbors

Taking or watching Holocaust testimony is a humbling experience.
Lawrence Langer, "The Alarmed Vision"

This Class and These Witnesses

In deciding to teach the Shoah, we made two firm decisions to which we have stayed true for nearly a decade: we would not show video of trauma and victimization, and we would rely heavily on survivor testimony. Indeed, for as long as possible, we would enlist the aid of living survivors to speak to our classes face-to-face about their war experiences but, facing the inevitable passing of survivors, we would rely on video and audio testimony. These two decisions would, at first glance, appear to be somewhat contradictory. After all, our decision not to show video of atrocity or its consequences grew out of a concern that we not victimize the victim further, that we not subject those who suffered so much to further indignity. And yet we have not spared survivors who, when recalling trauma for our benefit, reexperience the pain and loss of separation and often express deep anguish. Is that not victimizing the victim?

Of course, survivors have willingly—although at a great price—made themselves available to others, especially young people. Survivors generously bring to the surface the deep memory of trauma and loss in order to educate new generations about the wrongs of the past and to prevent such terrible events from reoccurring. We also recognize that when survivors resurrect the past, they are doing so through the mediation of language and their experience since the war. In other words, survivors are framing the terrible events of the Shoah in thoughtful and accessible ways, in ways that are safe and productive for our students. We do not believe that unmediated images of atrocity through film offer the same safety or frame.

We note other powerful advantages in using survivor testimony in the course, some obvious, others less so. We are struck by the personal nature of survivor testimony: the experience that is shared is the experience of a single person, whose life story, while resembling that of so many others, is indisputably unique to that individual. The Shoah is embodied in the life story of that individual rather than rendered as an abstraction (the six million Jews who perished or the twenty million Russians who lost their lives). Certainly, students engage history more readily when it is rendered as personalized experience—especially when that experience is rendered visually. And when students have the experience of seeing and listening to an actual survivor face-to-face, the degree of engagement is truly remarkable.

It may be obvious to most of us that eyewitness testimony given just after the event has special importance, as Yehuda Bauer's comments above imply. Shoah study depends on such testimony. The Nuremberg Trials, which attempted to document the atrocities committed during the Third Reich, wisely drew from survivors, for whom the pain was terribly fresh. For the historical record, the testimony of witnesses proves an indispensable part of the public record of those terrible events.

This is not to say that survivor testimony, even just after the event, is universally valued. In Jan Gross's *Neighbors,* we learn that the testimony of one Szmul Wasersztajn, an eyewitness to the wartime massacre of several hundred Jews by fellow townspeople of Jedwabne, was not regarded very seriously by historians and legal authorities. It required corroboration and could not stand on its own, so those experts said. Subsequently, what happened in Jedwabne on that terrible day in July 1941 would be swept under the rug (in a conspiracy by those who perpetrated the act and those who stood by, as well as by a Cold War calculation that this event was not worth accounting for) until some five decades after the fact. Perhaps, notes Gross, we should listen more attentively to the "lonely voices" (92).

Looking at and Not Merely through Testimony

While we wish our students to see witness testimony as an important part of the historical record, we see such testimony as providing important opportunity to discuss the way history is rendered and memory reconstructed. In other words, we invite students to examine survivor testimony historiographically and rhetorically. We ask that students read James E. Young's essay "Between History and Memory: The Uncanny Voices of Historian and Survivor" and consider the differences between the survivor's account of the past and that of the historian. In his reading journal for that week, Richard chooses to excerpt this passage from the Young essay, a passage that recounts a survivor's memory of a prisoner's revolt in Auschwitz:

> "All of a sudden . . . we saw four chimneys going up in flames, exploding. The flames shot into the sky, people were running. It was unbelievable." Unbelievable, indeed, retorted the historians who watched the tape, since only one chimney had been blown up. To their minds, such "flawed" testimony was as worthless to their inquiry into events as it was dangerous to historical truth. (538)

Young asserts that it would be a mistake to dismiss such testimony altogether. Rather, he argues for a reading of survivor accounts as records of emotional and psychological state as well as (to a degree) fact. It was the survivor's intense response to such an unlikely event that is noteworthy. Richard agrees and goes further in his commentary to insist that the historians are "naïve" in deeming the account "worthless." For him, the testimony is an expression of how history is rendered—and an expression of memory work:

> How could they not take a more personal approach and realize that such a traumatic event could build up dramatically when left in one's subconscious for such a long period of time? It is understandable that the historians care more for the "actual" historical events, but disregarding history and the impact it had on the woman that was an actual victim and survivor of Auschwitz . . . What is history but a representation of things that happened in a previous time through the memories of those who witnessed it? (Reading journal, March 2011)

In configuring history as a "representation" of the past, Richard continues to express a nascent awareness of disciplinary concerns. At the same time, he powerfully applies that awareness to elements of his experience outside of the classroom:

> Reading this reminded me of my foster sister, who had been raped on numerous occasions by her biological father. When she was a child she told her family what daddy had done to her, but as she grew older and attempted to pull those horrid memories from deep within, the story she told the courts changed slightly from the one family members had remembered her telling. With the minor discrepancies in her and the family's testimony, the loathsome degenerate only received two years in prison for his crimes. The "highly educated historians" showed similar disregard to this poor woman's experience. (Reading journal, March 2011)

These are strong and remarkably revealing words and speak to the power of testimony, here both received and offered (secondhand). Richard's largely emotional response to the passage from Young's essay shows genuine engagement with the problem of how to read a recollection of past trauma. Richard's view is that testimony born of trauma can "build up dramatically" and thus become something other than merely a regurgitation of fact. The psychological state of the witness is revealed through the "minor discrepancies." Persuaded by the "heartfelt testimony," Richard does not question the veracity of Young's paraphrase of the historians' judgment (Did they really feel that the account was "worthless"?), nor does Richard seem able to analyze these survivors' accounts on their own terms (Might we take the term "unbelievable" as a kind of gloss on the testimony—as "unbelievable" as four chimneys being blown up or as the fact of an uprising itself?). Rather, Richard focuses on extending the benefit of the doubt to the survivor.

Shoah scholars have presented us with various ways to analyze survivor testimony. Lawrence Langer, for example, deploys terms such as "chronological time" and "durational memory" to account for the discrepancy between the passing of time external to the survivor testimony and the persistent memory of loss (Langer, "Alarmed Vision" 57–58). Langer applies these terms to the testimony of one Bessie K., who lost her first family during the war, including a very young child, whom she had to give up to her Nazi captors. During video testimony, she sits next to her husband, with whom she started a second family. She observes that "since that time I think all my life I been alone" (Langer "Alarmed Vision" 57). Langer comments,

> [S]he is not complaining or asking for sympathy; she is explain-
> ing that the passage of time cannot appease a durational memory.
> She is redefining the meaning of being "alone, within myself,"
> making it a typical outgrowth of the disintegration of her first
> family, not to be undone by the emergence of a second one. The
> unappeasable experience is part of her inner reality, and, though
> the optimistic American temperament winces at the notion,
> Bessie K. knows that what she has survived is an event to be
> endured, not a trauma to be healed. ("Alarmed Vision" 57–58)

For Bessie K., the memory of loss exists in its own space and time, irrespective of external chronology (poignantly represented by her husband, with whom she sits "on the opposite ends of the couch" [Langer, "Alarmed Vision" 56]). Perhaps the survivor who recounted the "unbelievable" sight of four chimneys (potent symbols of the iconic death camp Auschwitz) exploding was caught in a "durational moment," which was not to be revised over time.

Although we rarely see such a systematic analysis of witness testimony from our students, it is worth noting, again, the powerfully affective response that so many express toward testimony. Indeed, some are moved to offer their own powerful testimony. Stacey, whose grandmother had been a Shoah survivor, makes a case for the power of art to render survivors' emotions. She describes two paintings made by her grandmother:

> My grandmother once drew a painting of a pile of bodies lying naked, with a Nazi guard smiling behind the piles of bodies. She then drew another picture right beside the first picture. The second picture was of the smiling Nazi, now dead, and the naked prisoners standing behind the dead Nazi, all of them smiling. (Stacey, final exam, February 2011)

Stacey's remarks bring a fresh reminder that even as they are expected to draw as much as possible from survivor testimony, our students assume the role of witnesses themselves, passing along through anecdote and personal experience what they know of this tragic moment in world history.

In chapter 4, we posed the question of whether our students would adopt the role of bystander or of agent in relation to our course subject: Will they be passive as learners? Or will they be motivated to take charge of what they have learned? And if they own their learning, will they then act to use their new knowledge to confront prejudice whenever and wherever it occurs? It is our hope that, in those moments, our students will offer evidence in the form of the survivor accounts and of their own testimony.

Shards of Memory on the Ground: Working with Witness Testimony

What is added to our understanding of the past by eyewitness testimony? We address that question quite early in the course when we view Kurt Messerschmidt's testimony regarding two Nazis who

> forced this very old gentleman to pick up these tiny glass splinters one by one. . . . and they all were standing there and watching. . . . The only thing we could think of was to help. . . . We went down on our knees and started picking up one by one. . . . I looked at the two guys and they didn't blink, didn't move. Why

didn't they move? . . . I know that some of the people there dis-
approved of what the Nazis did, but their disapproval was only
silence—and silence is what did the harm. (Messerschmidt)

As we have seen, this episode speaks powerfully to the consequences
of inaction—leaving the old man to pick up the shards all by himself—and of engagement—the two young men share the burden of
picking up the glass fragments, thus relieving the old man of some of
that task. But we learn more from Mr. Messerschmidt's account than
this somewhat obvious fact. Our students note—with Messerschmidt
decades removed from the event—his disbelief (then and now) that
people would simply stand around the old man and do nothing (one
student used the term "callousness" to describe the spectators) (class
transcript, February 2011). If we keep in mind that Messerschmidt
is recalling emotion and thought from the vantage point of having
learned, after the fact, of the terrible atrocities committed during the
war, his disbelief, so clearly expressed through tone and affect, is simply astonishing. Naturally, we would expect the retrospective view
that this indifference to another's degradation and suffering was all too
predictive of what would follow in other places. But Messerschmidt is
not merely thinking about this scene as part of a larger context: he is
calling upon the same emotions that he felt when, at the age of twenty-
four, he witnessed this local and shameful episode. The passion felt
then Messerschmidt feels once more.

Our students note as well the emotion of surprise that character-
izes Messerschmidt's account of this moment: "no one got in the way"
of his and his friend's helping the old man (class transcript, February
2011). "Why didn't they blink?" asks Messerschmidt. The surprise that
he felt then emerges even now. It implies the expectation, then, that
the Brownshirts (Nazi SA) would act to stop the young men, perhaps
by inflicting humiliation on them, too. The absence of any kind of
retaliation from the Nazis—indeed, of any action at all—suggests an
extremely potent message: that resistance to power—in this case, the
power to order the humiliation of the old man—might prove powerful in its own way. If no punishment was meted out to the young
men, what might have happened if the entire group had done the same
and assisted the old man? It is impossible not to infer this message,

given Messerschmidt's own words and the expression of surprise in his tone and facial expression. Did Messerschmidt offer a comprehensive account of what happened that night in Berlin? Obviously not—after all, how much could two excited young men on bicycles in a vast city really see? But in localizing and concretizing this catastrophe he does us an immeasurable service: he humanizes this tragedy and renders it, if not comprehensible, at least accessible to us.

We respond to the testimony of Shoah witnesses, especially of survivors, in extremes. On the one hand, we endow them, according to one of our students, with a kind of "sanctity" (Samantha, reading journal, March 2011). The witnesses bear a heavy burden of recounting terrible pain. We are inclined, then, not to subject their testimony to study and critique—out of respect or out of an unwillingness to inflict further pain. On the other hand, we may be inclined to question much of a witness's account, in part because of its very human and fallible perspective. To find the right balance—between a respect for the integrity of the witness account and a reasonable questioning of that account—is part of our students' journey in this course. We like to think of the challenge as finding a harmonious relationship between the cognitive and affective response to Shoah testimony. This is a journey of learning, one that requires time and patience to complete. Samantha puts it well—and this is a realization that occurs to her in the second half of the semester: "Acknowledging the faults and frailty of human memory should not demean its sanctity; on the contrary, memory's inability to achieve perfection should be seen as a reflection of the human condition itself, and by extension a 'pure' form of humanity's interconnectedness" (reading journal, March 2011). To view witness testimony as "imperfect" seems a wise and practical move, acknowledging the very real limits of such testimony, all the while respecting the act of bearing witness and thus maintaining the "connectedness" between the historical and current moment.

We have various other opportunities to hear survivor testimony via videotape. In an effort to show our students what it was like to disembark at a concentration camp, we watch the testimony of Ellis Lewin, who describes the first moments of his family's arrival in Auschwitz: "When we arrived at Auschwitz, . . . it was like you open the doors and you find yourself in this inferno," with dogs barking, commands shouted (n. pag.). Everything moved so quickly: it was all part of the design, says Lewin, to stun those coming to the camp. His mother and sister were then separated from Lewin and his father: "I never got to say goodbye to my mother; I never got to say goodbye to my sister" (n. pag.). Lewin was put into the line with the men. He could not hold onto his father, since, according to Lewin, the Nazis aimed at destroying families. He had to behave as if he were on his own.

Why do we show this video? Certainly, students will have read about and seen films that dramatized the cattle cars, barking dogs, the disposal of prisoners' belongings, and the separation of men from women and children, young from old. The commentary that Mr. Lewin provides as to the Nazis' motives behind the shock and awe, or the destruction of family, likely reflect research that Mr. Lewin had done after the fact. What justifies our viewing of this testimony transcends the merely factual. This is how Samantha, commenting on witness testimony generally, puts the matter:

> First hand accounts have with them an image burned into the psyche of the person telling their tale; the image can be physical, visual, aural, or even spiritual. This image of subjective value is integral in helping generations otherwise unaffected by the Shoah understand the magnitude and human element of the genocide. (Reading journal, March 2011)

When Mr. Lewin recounts that moment of disembarking from the cattle car, his eyes reflect that searing image of the inferno into which he and his family had stumbled. The look retains the devastation and fear from that time so long ago. Our students must work to recognize and understand this image of subjective value. It will not come of its own to them. They must be ready to receive it. They must be ready to witness and to bear witness.

Looking through the Peephole: Seeing and Yet Unseen

Among the video testimony that we view in the course, none is more poignant and revealing than that of John S., a Jesuit priest who lived and trained at a seminary in occupied Hungary during the war.

In his testimony, John recounts a time he observed through the peep-hole of a wooden fence the loading of a cattle car with Jews at a railroad station. He had heard that Nazis were armed with machine guns ready to intercept anyone who approached the fence. But he admits that it was his "discipline," his role in the seminary, that caused him to hesitate, since he was entrusted to go to the city to buy something. He "sneaked up" to the fence anyway, and didn't see soldiers or anyone for that matter. "That was the day that I saw *my train*" ("John S"; italics ours). It quickly becomes obvious that over the years this moment has become, in his own words, his personal encounter with the Shoah. This is his train, his moment. Would he be ready to meet the challenge? The train's door opened and what he saw was "terrifying"—so many people packed together, mothers with their children. He saw a man jump off the train and seemingly ask a soldier ("politely") for some water. Immediately, the soldier took his rifle and struck the man, "several times, to insensitivity." John then ran away, upset and scared. He would on another occasion hear wailing in the night—wailing from Jews, as he was told. What follows is truly extraordinary:

> I see this personally as the greatest tragedy of my life. Jewish people were deported around me—I didn't do anything. I panicked, not even fear. I just didn't know what to do. . . . I didn't know about the "death camps" [he uses air quotes around the phrase]. I didn't know about the ovens, the burning. But personally I felt the persuasion coming over me that these people would be killed. . . . I wish I could relive my life. Today, maybe, I would be ready to run in front of the train and lay down. Maybe today I would call out or protest or risk being shot down or clubbed down. . . . It was utterly beyond my experience. I was utterly unprepared.

John's discomfort at his own failure to act, so evident after all these years, provides our students with a complicating factor when assessing the burden of the witness, in this case a witness who comes forward only decades after the fact (the testimony was filmed in 1985). Inaction carries its own consequences, not only for the victim and perpetrator (we surmise), but for the passive observer. We cannot refer to John S. as indifferent, surely, because he carries the scar of his personal encounter with the Shoah. But we can and should acknowledge the moral and physical paralysis that took hold of him—the sense of not knowing how to act when he was completely unprepared. That acknowledgment of not being prepared rings hollow, for who could have been prepared for the atrocities that were being witnessed on a daily basis?

John S.'s tormented struggles, after decades, to reconcile his past inaction with the teachings of his church—in whose service he has devoted his life—provides a rather dramatic counterpoint to our students' query, noted often in the previous chapter, "Why didn't people do more?" John S. reminds us that to the witness the question of what actions were available plays a secondary role to the durational moment characterizing so much of witness testimony. This moment continues tantalizingly and painfully as the ongoing present, even as the judgment of posterity weighs heavily on the witness.

Witness as Spectacle

As dramatic as such video testimony can be, we and our students were hardly prepared to encounter the live testimony offered by Mr. Steven Ross, survivor of ten camps, who came to speak to our class and to the college community in the latter part of the semester. For several years our students had had the opportunity to listen to survivors live. Invariably, we and our students are moved by what we hear and by the affect of the survivor, for whom testimony brings back deep memory in painful ways. We concur with Omer Bartov, who notes that these accounts, "fraught and painful and contradictory as they are, constitute a crucial component of the past" (27). Yet it must also be said that we—ourselves and our students—tend to listen and watch live survivor testimony somewhat uncritically. We regard them as merely the direct delivery of firsthand, lived experience, rather than a constructed performance. We recall vividly a kind of choreography during one visit with a survivor: after telling a harrowing story of deprivation and his own near-death experience in a camp, the survivor rolled up his sleeve to reveal the number tattooed on his arm, a gesture timed to have the maximum effect on his audience, which indeed it had. At the time, given the powerfully emotional impact of the survivor's story, none of us, it is safe to say, marked the deliberate nature of that move.

It seems obvious to say that when we all entered a large theater and saw Mr. Ross dressed in what was clearly a camp inmate's uniform, a uniform that Mr. Ross proudly claimed he had purchased in a Boston department store for such an event as this, we were all taken aback. The uniform signaled to us an aspect of performance in Mr. Ross's presentation, although many in attendance, including our students, were quite stirred emotionally by the talk, rather than inclined to offer a critique of the testimony as performance. It was a stunning sight, to be sure: a survivor of the camps willingly putting on the symbols of his own pain and devastation. We are reminded of the moment in Art Spiegelman's *Maus*, when, having been restored to health after liberation, Vladek, wanting a souvenir before reuniting with his wife after such a long and terrifying separation, dons a new, crisp uniform, steps into a photo booth, and has a photograph taken of himself, with cap jauntily angled. Spiegelman makes it clear throughout *Maus* how flamboyant Vladek's personality was—as a young man, as a camp inmate, and even late in life. Still, this photograph is startling in Vladek's attempt to appropriate the symbol of his suffering for ends other than what the perpetrators intended. Perhaps Vladek, like Mr. Ross, wishes to assert some control over his own past.

Not only did Mr. Ross wear the uniform of his enslavement, but he also brought various props—including a metal soup bowl, animal figures made out of the bones of Jewish prisoners, and the top of a sardine can. Aided by these props, Mr. Ross told a harrowing story: he described the time when he eluded the selection process by hiding in an outhouse, covered up to his neck in feces and urine; he talked of drinking soup that was little more than brown water infested with cockroaches; and he observed that he and a group of twenty men had to survive each night on a single slice of bread. Unlike the survivors whom we had heard in the past and who were understated in describing the conditions that they faced—choosing instead to focus on the psychological challenges of loss—Mr. Ross highlighted those conditions, by rendering them as graphically as one could imagine. Moreover, he spoke openly of two experiences that by themselves set his oral testimony apart from that of others: cannibalism and rape. Starving, Mr. Ross and fellow inmates followed the lead of Russian prisoners and ate the flesh of the dead (using the tops of sardine cans to peel off the flesh). Moreover, Mr. Ross revealed women "sold themselves" for a piece of bread, and that he himself was a victim of rape in the camps. Barely sixty pounds at liberation, Mr. Ross had suffered from tuberculosis and a broken back (dealt by a guard when Mr. Ross sought some food).

Certainly those in attendance felt the power of Mr. Ross's testimony. Richard, a student whose words we have drawn from often in this study, was particularly affected by the experience. In his final exam, when asked what, if anything, he had to "unlearn" from taking this course, Richard pointed to this experience of listening to a survivor:

> Steven Ross will be forever ingrained in my memory. Before he spoke, I assumed it would be like telling any story that anyone has told a thousand times; I was dead wrong. He told us about being born in urine, hiding in urine and feces, washing in urine, and how he can still smell it to this day. I was overcome with emotions. His numerous attempts of holding back his tears as he accounts for the 3500 Jews that were killed in 3 minutes in the gas chambers, of the numerous rapes that he encountered whenever he would get water, truly showed me the power that deep memory holds. (Final exam, May 2011)

We wish that we could probe further what Richard means when he refers to "any story . . . told a thousand times." Is he suggesting that previous video testimony seems as if it had been told and retold, perhaps too smoothly presented, despite the painful subject matter? Perhaps. We wish that Richard had been able to articulate more clearly that difference. However, we can certainly infer that the dramatic display of outward emotion from a survivor who had seen and experienced such atrocity accounts at least in part for that difference. The struggle to retrieve that "deep memory" was all too evident to everyone in the room. And, clearly, Richard is swayed by the graphic, visceral detail that marked Mr. Ross's performance.

The sensational nature of that detail leaves Mr. Ross open to charges of inflating the facts (indeed, a cursory Google search quickly brings up a charge of "hoax"), despite evidence attesting to cannibalism and sexual assaults in the camps (*Exposing;* "Wöbbelin"; "Flossenburg"; Morrissette). But the point that we wish to make is not that Mr. Ross was wrong or even showing bad taste in representing his Shoah experience so graphically. Rather, we wonder why there is so little evidence of a critical response in Richard's statement to Mr. Ross's presentation. We certainly do not wish Richard to question the veracity of Mr. Ross's memory but wonder why he does not put Mr. Ross's testimony within the context of other testimony or regard Mr. Ross's rhetorical appeal to the audience's emotions (deploying pathos).

Spectacle aside, Mr. Ross's presentation drew a significant amount of its power from the trauma that lay at the heart of the experience described, including his own rape. We naturally wonder what happens when such deeply felt trauma is communicated to our students. Students encounter many scenes of atrocity in class readings: What is their response when reading such scenes? Does such atrocity stop them in their tracks? And if so, what are they thinking during that pause? What questions come up? Are they able to continue to read as if this moment were like any other in the reading? Or are they compelled to stop reading altogether? Is critique possible, when the subject is trauma?

6 ▪ Trauma

"They chased them all to a barn. Poured kerosene all around. It took but two minutes, but the scream . . . I can still hear it. . . . They were so intertwined with one another that bodies could not be disentangled," recalled an elderly peasant, who, as a young boy, had been sent with a group of local men to bury the dead.

Jan T. Gross, Neighbors

As told by Adam Wilma, the bodies of the dead were described as roots of a tree. The description of bodies is inhumane accounting the same for the inhumane treatments the Jews were treated with. This quote was very hard for me to read since I have a very vivid imagination when the author describes the way (directionally) the fire had spread and the tormented souls within the barn piling up together at their, at that moment, inevitable death.

Stefane, reading journal, March 2011

Is there a relationship between crisis and the very enterprise of education? To put the question even more audaciously and bluntly: Is there a relationship between trauma and pedagogy? . . . Can trauma instruct pedagogy, and can pedagogy shed light on the mystery of trauma?

Shoshana Felman, "Education and Crisis, or the Vicissitudes of Teaching" 13

Blaming (or Ignoring) the Messenger of Trauma

When we first talked of designing a course on the Shoah for our community college's honors program, the two of us wondered about the cost, both to ourselves and to our students. We feared becoming too emotionally invested in stories of unbelievable loss and cruelty, especially given that for Howard, a child of Shoah survivors, such accounting might very well recall the loss that his parents knew—of parents, grandparents, siblings, and cousins, all murdered during the Shoah. But we also regarded our students with some concern, since so many who come to our community college have suffered some kind of trauma themselves—such as the loss of friends and family members, or the dislocation caused by unemployment—and who have battled to recover their equilibrium ever since. Despite Goldenberg's assertion, noted earlier, that community colleges are prime places in which to insert the Shoah into the general education curriculum, we harbored deep reservations about doing so at our college. What good could come of showing suffering to students who had witnessed more than their share?

We continue to treat that as a serious question, deserving of some serious problem solving. Although our intention is never to seek "good" from anyone's pain, we think it possible that we and our students may learn something, to use Shoshana Felman's term, from the "mystery of trauma" (1). We are intrigued by Felman's assumption that teaching can draw strength from crisis and trauma. Certainly we have observed over the years that those students who stay the course, as it were, form tight bonds with each other. They become witnesses themselves. But there is no denying the pain that comes with such a role.

We have already seen how reading about Shoah atrocities can call forth from our students traumas of their own or of those whom they love—Richard recalling the abuse suffered by his foster sister and Stacey painfully reprising her grandmother's artistic rendering of loss during the war. But we speculate as to whether our students are likely to respond to trauma with some distance or perhaps even denial. Some students simply have been unable to read through difficult passages and are stopped in their tracks. Others offer an empathetic response to the pain described. Still others choose to distance themselves through critical analysis rather than empathy. Finally, and most intriguingly, there are those who attempt to find a balance between distance and proximity, critical analysis and empathy. In this chapter, we will attempt to show the full range of student response to trauma.

Before doing so, however, we want to mention a striking moment in one of our students' journals. It is week eight of our course. Stefane and her classmates have just finished reading Jan Gross's *Neighbors*, which provides a wartime case study of the Polish town of Jedwabne, the site of a pogrom, or massacre. The events reach their climax when Jewish men, women, and children are locked in a barn that is then set on fire, killing all within. One student, Stefane, expresses difficulty when reading the graphic description of the victims' charred remains—a response that is certainly understandable. But what strikes us as unusual is this part: "The description of bodies is inhumane accounting the same for the inhuman treatments the Jews were treated with" (Stefane, reading journal, March 2011). Despite the awkward (and repetitive) phrasing, we note one observation: Stefane seems to find that the description afforded by the witness (and by Gross, presumably) amounts to an "inhumane" representation. In other words, she seems to be saying that the description itself ought to have been withheld, since her "vivid imagination" makes the experience of reading the passage quite painful—and, she may be implying, the victims themselves might have been spared such recounting of their terrible end. While the latter point is important, raising as it does the whole problem of victimizing the victims through an unseemly display of their fate, it is to the first point that we want to direct our attention here. In essence, she blames the messenger for delivering or reproducing an unbelievable image of atrocity, a response the kind of which Szmul Wasersztajn, one of the few surviving witnesses to the pogrom, received when deposed just after the war (Gross 6).

There Is No Reasoning: When Images of Atrocity Stop Us in Our Tracks

As we continue to analyze our students' responses to the trauma of the Shoah, we become aware of an impulse simply to stop engaging the material, acknowledging that no amount of reason or analysis can bring us closer to understanding how this atrocity was possible. Stefane, once again, provides a case in point. As we indicate in chapter 4, Stefane responds intensely to a scene in Ida Fink's short story "A Spring Morning," specifically to the father's "pointless" efforts to save his child (Stefane, reading journal, February 2011). And now the father and mother must endure additional pain and suffering as they march to their own inevitable death. We note the lack of graphic detail in the description: Fink's restraint merely highlights the suffering of the victims but it also stands in contrast with Stefane's unrestrained expression of helplessness when confronted with the scene:

> *There is no understanding* how this could have possibly happened, *there is no way* someone can even read about this terrible story and not shed a tear. . . . All the assigned readings for this week were very strong and graphic to me and surely to all that have read these passages before. Abraham Lewin's "Diary of the Great Deportation" the fact that it is a diary and you knew from his words, feelings, and point that it would be possible [*sic*] to add any more details because *these details cannot be explained*, or worded. Everything that Lewin describes are events that happened around him, the numbness he started to feel toward the end of his diary excerpts made it possible for me to continue [as] the reader, if not for that his feelings would have been more prominent in his words and therefore I would not stop my tears from coming. (Reading journal, February 2011; italics ours)

Student disengagement is rarely a problem in this course: students are engaged thoroughly by what they read and discuss. Indeed that engagement leads to genuine discomfort and, as in Stefane's case, emotional exposure. Superficially, we might observe the problem to be too much engagement, but that is really not the case. Rather, a kind of shutting down of both the reading and reflecting processes occur. The phrases in Stefane's commentary that we have italicized reveal a lack of faith in language and reason to encompass such pain. We note earlier that Stefane came to our class not knowing, by her own admission, much about the Shoah, having gleaned what she knew about the subject from the film *Schindler's List*. As powerful as that film is, Lewin's on-the-ground, real life reporting of the Warsaw Ghetto's liquidation becomes too personal—both to Lewin himself (who must report the loss of his wife and then his daughter) and to Stefane. Moreover, Ida Fink's story, while fictional, is rendered with such understated power it is hardly surprising, then, that Stefane would be stopped in her tracks. It is also not surprising that when asked to reflect on how the reading has broadened her understanding of the Shoah, Stefane, recalling not only the work of the Nazis but also Ukrainians, Poles, and Jewish police in perpetrating atrocities, refers to such perpetrators not as humans "but instead demons" (reading journal, February 2011). As we observed earlier, Stefane seems almost to be waving the flag of surrender: the Shoah surpasses our understanding. These were not men; these were devils. In making such a claim, Stefane does not offer a reasoned explanation of the perpetrators' actions. She does not attempt to theorize the reasons behind these men's actions: that they were blinded by ideology, that they were persuaded by virulent antisemitism to objectify their victims, or that they were ordinary men who managed to do the things that they did by compartmentalizing their cruel acts, as some have noted (Goldhagen; Browning; Lifton). For Stefane, atrocity carries no rationale, or invitation to speculate as to causes. It is simply too painful to consider.

Empathy's End

In contrast to a shutting down when faced with Shoah trauma, we note among some students an altogether easy empathy when confronted with such trauma. We note, again in stark contrast with a turning of one's gaze away from the pain, an almost lingering, sometimes even curious stare. Indeed, such a response seems at times to be almost unfeeling, as one Shoah scholar has termed it—as if empathy itself becomes the price to be paid for our fascination with images of atrocity and other people's trauma (Dean). For example, a number of students have expressed a desire to present evidence of Nazi experimentation on camp prisoners in their end-of-semester digital research projects. We have rejected such proposals, offering as one rationale that such presentations would dishonor and degrade the victims. But we cannot help notice the ongoing fascination with images of trauma:

hence our decision to forgo video that would in essence feed that fascination.

Yet we cannot entirely escape culpability ourselves. After all, we ask students to read a work that contains testimony such as this: "Jakub Kac they stoned to death with bricks. Krawiecki they knifed and then plucked his eyes and cut off his tongue. He suffered terribly for twelve hours before he gave up his soul" (Gross 3). What kind of response to this testimony do we wish to elicit from our students? Are our expectations influenced by our own subjectivities? In that regard, we note our own family connection (Howard's maternal and paternal grandparents and external family having resided and no doubt perished near this town) to the events in occupied southeastern Poland, where Ukrainians "massacred about 4,000 Jews" in the town of Lvov in July 1941 ("Lvov"). Later that month, a second pogrom (Petliura Days) took place, again conducted by Ukrainians who "took groups of Jews to the Jewish Cemetery and to Lunecki prison and shot them" ("Lvov"). In that attack "more than 2000 Jews were murdered" ("Lvov"). We can safely assume that many of Howard's family members were among the "more than 2000."

Might we, thus entangled with and moved by the tragic events at the time and of that place, expect students to feel as we do, to put themselves in the position of those who suffered so? Might we expect a pull, a tug of the heartstrings, just as we feel when reading of such trauma? Might we expect compassion and empathy for those victimized? Many years ago, one of our students confided in us that she and many of her classmates felt as if they were "walking on eggshells" when discussing various aspects of the Shoah, knowing that at least one of us had suffered the loss of so many family members during the war. Was our pain so visible to our students? Have we made the Shoah *our* Holocaust, to the extent that our students fear either identifying with our pain or questioning it in some way? We have yet to arrive at an answer to these questions.

Many of our students, despite such concerns, seem to feel and express a degree of empathy toward Shoah victims, as we have seen. "I am there when I read this passage," comments Andreea, in response to a moment in Charlotte Delbo's "Voices," when a woman in a camp holds her dead sister: "I am behind this woman, watching her hold her dying sister, wishing she as well would die. I can feel her guilt for being alive" (reading journal, February 2011). We are struck both by Andreea's earnest effort to feel for the woman but also by the artificial construction of her response. As she interjects herself into the scene, Andreea attempts to transform herself from bystander to participant but instead simply asserts a relationship to the scene rather than evoking emotion. She may claim to "feel" the woman's "guilt," but that feeling is hardly evident in the language offered. Indeed, the language "gives away" the artifice, as Andreea "watches" the woman, seemingly "wishing" she would die. We see no evidence beyond the assertion of such empathy. That assertion seems, well, too easy.

In our students' defense, perhaps the Shoah makes empathy virtually impossible. Note that we do not imply the inevitability of a kind of jaded response to Shoah trauma (in the age of digitized violence) or the dismissal of the Shoah and genocides that follow as "other people's holocausts" (Jay). Rather, as our most astute students have taught us, we theorize that efforts to empathize with Shoah victims need to be accompanied by a recognition of empathy's limits—and the awareness that one's relationship to the Shoah is never really quite stable or sure. Primo Levi's experience seems particularly apt:

> I described the public hanging of a resistor before a terrified and apathetic crowd of prisoners. This is a thought that barely grazed us, but that returned "afterward": you too could have, you certainly should have. And this is a judgment that the Survivor believes he sees in the eyes of those (especially the young) who listen to his stories and judge with facile hindsight. (112)

Levi writes from the unique perspective of a survivor of trauma, one who should be spared the judgment from someone who "jests at scars, never having felt a wound" (Shakespeare, 2.2.1). Yet Levi also invites our students to consider the uneasy apathy that, mingled with terror, stalls efforts to empathize with those who suffer. Interestingly, Samantha, who seems particularly struck by Levi's remarks, reciprocates with a defense of Levi and of her own self-interest (as a young person):

> It *hurts* me that Mr. Levi feels that he sees judgment and a cruel repulsion especially in the eyes of the young, because after going through an experience as he did nobody should be subject to judgment. (Reading journal, February 2011)

It "hurts" Samantha, as a young person, to be singled out as a group likely to find fault with Levi's inaction (and apparent lack of feeling) as the resistor is hanged. Yet it also "hurts" Samantha that Levi would be judged unfairly: "judgment should be reserved for those who perpetrated the crimes (and even then withheld to an extent) in order to preserve the integrity of the sufferer's experience" (reading journal, February 2011). Her effort to enter into the "sufferer's experience" seems especially noteworthy, given her acknowledgment that the "integrity" of that experience be respected at all costs, even at the price of withholding judgment of the perpetrators themselves. Respecting that integrity does not, however, prevent her from attempting to feel something of what it was like to be in the survivor's place: "I have often tried to place myself in the shoes of a Shoah survivor and find it utterly impossible." Why try, if that is the inevitable outcome? The answer to that question, Samantha implies, may lie in the paradox that defines survivor testimony and, we infer, reader reception of that testimony:

> Paradoxically, the fact that a Shoah survivor feels the need to justify and defend him or herself is a very positive aspect of the shame felt by survivors. Perhaps without the need to justify and defend themselves Shoah survivors would be less likely to present accounts of their plight, and as a result the world [would] be less informed of the very real human experience of the Shoah. (Reading journal, February 2011)

Although we are not prepared to view guilt or a need to justify their behavior as a motive for survivors' sharing testimony, we regard Samantha's construction of the paradox as quite resourceful and useful, building upon the paradox that Levi himself constructs: the terror and apathy that he and other observers experienced. But we see additional ramifications from Samantha's calculation. Just as survivors may feel compelled to offer testimony even as they fear repulsion and judgment, so, too, an audience for such testimony may feel the need to engage narratives of trauma despite an awareness that empathy is not achievable. In other words, Samantha and others attempt empathy not to achieve that outcome as much as to give tribute to the survivor and to the "complexity of the Shoah and its aftermath . . . [an outcome that adds to their] ever changing image of the Shoah" (reading journal, February 2011). Samantha's insights into the similarity between reader and survivor of trauma do not stop here, however. After listening to another student, Hillary, express the view that survivor testimony must be seen as unique to that individual even as it speaks for others, Samantha reveals her own "shame": "During this journal I was guilty of viewing the guilt and shame felt by Shoah survivors as one, instead of different and varying, as I should have" (reading journal, February 2011). What she now views as a weakness on her part, we regard as a strength: her sensitivity to the power and poignancy of Levi's testimony. Knowing that she can never truly feel the trauma that confronts survivors, we are confident that she will make the effort nonetheless to engage that trauma fully, despite the inevitable failure. Her practice of seeing all survivor trauma summed up in the one account, together with her own empathic imagination, compels her to make that effort.

Samantha is not alone in pursuing the impulse to empathize, despite the obstacles to doing so. It could be said that the entire work *Maus* represents Art Spiegelman's attempt to empathize with his father, Vladek, whose Shoah experiences are recounted in the graphic novel. Try as he might, Art is reminded often by Vladek how fruitless that effort is likely to be. Art's complaint to his father early in the novel about being left behind by his friends receives this reply from Vladek: "Friends? Your friends? If you lock them together in a room with no food for a week[,] THEN you could see what it is, friends." (*Maus I* 6) The fact that Art is but "ten or eleven" appears irrelevant to Vladek, who feels compelled to remind Art that Shoah trauma will remain impenetrable to Art and that such trauma will always stand as a point of reference for all pain and shame. Later in the work, Vladek reminds his son, now an adult, that try however he might, Art "can't know what it is, to be hungry" (*Maus II* 91). Hillary, the student with whom Samantha has an exchange, sees much to be learned from this last comment. She notes that Vladek offers evidence of his own "present-mindedness" (Spiegelman, "Making of Maus"). Vladek is merely emphasizing how he "used food as a long-lasting survival tactic," bartering for goods at a time of extreme scarcity (reading journal, April 2011). But then Hillary offers up this surprise:

> Reading deeper into the text, I noticed that this passage is directed toward someone. In context, Vladek is talking to his son, Art. However, I believe that Art included it because it is directed to everyone who tries to empathize with the survivors. The fact of the matter is, we can sympathize, but being able to fully empathize is nearly impossible. (Reading journal, April 2011)

The distinction between sympathy and empathy is not the surprising element here: it is a logical distinction, to be sure, but, as Art continually reminds the reader, Vladek neither conveys much sympathy nor elicits it from others. More interesting to us is that Hillary can discern the author's attention (Art's motives as writer): he has Vladek put a "stop sign" in front of all of us when we try to get close to wartime trauma. Hillary, moreover, shows explicit awareness of her own reading process, distinguishing between this deeper reading and the surface reading that precedes it. In so doing, she expresses metacognitive capability, which we reference in chapter 3 as a key element of disciplinary and integrative knowledge. For our purposes here, however, it is what Hillary writes next that provides the greater revelation:

> The first part says that we can't know. It's true. I will never know how it feels to walk by people who were once my neighbors now hanging in the trees. I will never know what it is like to have my humanity stripped from me, to be treated no longer as a person. I can't feel lice in my bed, infection in my body, or dead bodies under my feet. I don't know what fear actually is. (Reading journal, April 2011)

Hillary's explicit intention—to affirm the limits of empathy—could not be any clearer. She replies to Vladek's assertion in the affirmative: "It's true." But her phrasing—her skillful use of rhetoric—conveys a different message. The insistent repetition of phrases and sentence structure ("I will never know. . . . I will never know. . . . I can't feel. . . . I don't know") and the appeal to emotion via evocative detail ("neighbors hanging in the trees," "lice in my bed") suggest a heart and not just a mind at work. Like Samantha, Hillary makes the effort to empathize despite the impossibility of achieving that end. "I have often tried to place myself in the shoes of a Shoah survivor," writes Samantha (reading journal, February 2011). She is not alone.

Critiquing Trauma from a Distance: A *Maus* Trap

Empathy requires proximity, or at least a reaching out toward the object with which we aspire to empathize. As if to promote a different kind of understanding, many of the writers whose work we discuss during the semester attempt to give our students a view of the Shoah from the periphery. Aharon Appelfeld's novella *Tzili* intentionally forgoes any glimpse of camp or ghetto life. Rather, Appelfeld wishes to depict the impact of the Shoah through the life of an abandoned young girl, who survives the Shoah in the forest. We do see Tzili being cruelly and unfairly beaten, but we do not witness the trauma associated with the ghetto or camp at the point of attack. Instead the pain is communicated after the fact, and we often experience it through a character's sense of profound loss or through evocative objects. We wonder whether our students will engage the literature of trauma when the evidence of such trauma is delivered tangentially. Here is a case in point: Mark, a survivor who leaves his wife and children behind in a camp, tends to the washing of his children's clothes, under Tzili's (and the reader's) watchful eye:

> Strange his nervousness was not apparent now. He stood next to the steaming clothes, turning them over one by one, as if they were pieces of meat on a fire. Tzili too did not take her eyes off the stained children's clothes shrinking in the sun. (Appelfeld 301)

If this scene were made into a film, we would be escorted back to the camp to witness the inevitable death of the children, in graphic brutality. Appelfeld provides an insight into the children's fate and its impact on Mark much more subtly, challenging the reader to grasp the figurative meaning. Stefane, for one, is up to the challenge:

> [The passage] seems to be symbolizing what is truly happening
> outside the forest. The clothes to me act to symbolize the bod-
> ies of Mark's family, the author chose to even refer to them as
> "pieces of meat on a fire," juxtaposing the bodies of his family
> in the crematorium. It acts to foreshadow what is really going
> to happen to those who once wore those pieces of clothing.
> (Reading journal, March 2011)

This moment of deep reading manages at once to convey Stefane's
emotional connection to Mark's tragic predicament while at the same
time deploying a useful interpretive frame on the passage. The dan-
ger that Appelfeld faces in placing the Shoah at the margins is that
readers may either lose interest (Stefane finds Tzili's naïveté "frustrat-
ing" [reading journal, March 2011]) and turn away from the work, or
engage it purely as an intellectual matter. We believe that Stefane has
found a happy medium between empathy and critique. She couples
this last passage, by the way, with another and even more poignant line
spoken by Mark: "Death will follow us all our lives" (Appelfeld 322).
The two passages taken together allow Stefane to demonstrate her
sensitivity to the emotion conveyed while at the same time drawing
from Stefane a synthetic interpretation: she is able to bring together in
meaningful ways a whole host of "objective correlatives," as it were:
the camp, the children, the stains in their clothes, the firing of the
ovens and, of course, Mark's own tortured guilt.

Interestingly, and in dialogue with Stefane, Samantha offers a take
on this moment in the novel that creates a broader context, a somewhat
deeper interpretation and a more complex synthesis, than Stefane's.
The passage that she couples with the passage about the clothing
is this: "When she awoke, her memory was empty and weightless"
(Appelfeld 277). The commentary that follows refuses to be bound by
the scene or by Mark's traumatic memory:

> [T]he second passage seems to stand in contrast to the first
> because Mark is standing next to the clothes of his children and
> seemingly remembering, or reflecting back on, his life before
> the war. Mark's memories calmed him, whereas Tzili's lack of
> memory calmed her. The image of steaming children's clothes
> shrinking in the sun could be symbolic of Mark's children's

souls and lives leaving the physical realm and becoming part of something greater, and burning themselves forever into Mark's memory. It is interesting to me that Tzili is the one who has been freed of her memories while Mark, who was in the camps and witnessed firsthand the horrors of the Shoah, is tormented by them and ultimately finds his demise in them. Tzili's ability (be it a gift or a curse) to forget the concrete memories of her past seems to help her cope and detach herself from the world around [and] help her survive in an extremely hostile environment and time. (Samantha, reading journal, March 2011)

By placing memory, and Tzili's buried version of it, at the center of her reading, Samantha expands the reach of this passage considerably. Her commentary serves to remind us that there are many ways in which to confront past trauma. Mark's all-too-clear intention to end his own life is not the only path open to him. He can, in the memorable figure used by another of our authors, Charlotte Delbo, take "leave of [his] skin . . . and [find himself] another, beautiful and clean" (Delbo 77). He can bury his memory deep enough so as to carry on. Samantha's reading, in addition to showing this alternative path, brings us back to the central character of the novel, Tzili, through whose consciousness the story is told. Sometimes the least likely paths are the truest. And sometimes the most meek among us are the most likely to prevail in time of loss.

Perhaps it might also be said that the "mystery of trauma" (to use Felman's term once more) is best unraveled from a distance. The point is brought home late in the semester by Samantha, when she offers commentary on a scene from *Maus* in which Vladek recounts being brought to Auschwitz (*Maus I* 157). Samantha chooses not to focus on the barking dogs, the cramped conditions in the transport, the looming hunger. In fact, she confides that she has chosen this set of panels "not for emotional reasons" (reading journal, April 2011). That declaration signals to us that she will attempt to distance herself from the emotionally laden scene in favor of an interpretive stance. In so doing, she is enabled by Art Spiegelman's method in the graphic memoir, a work that figures the Shoah using animal characters in the comic genre—with the effect of making trauma a safe subject with which to engage. Instead of attempting a purely empathic response,

Samantha discerns a dissonance between this passage and her prior understanding:

> First of all, when Vladek arrives at Auschwitz he says that he knew what kind of place it was and what happened there. This is almost at odds with other first-hand accounts (like Abraham Lewin's diary from the Warsaw ghetto) about what the Jews knew about the concentration and extermination camps before they were deported. In Lewin's diary, he says that stories about the camps came back to the Jews in the ghetto; [they] didn't really know what to think about them, although they were frightened. (Reading journal, April 2011)

This seems to be a significant moment for Samantha—and a telling instance of effective learning. She acknowledges that the image of the camp as presented in the panel is "in keeping" with what she has "seen and read beforehand" (reading journal, April 2011). And she is able to declare her prior understanding that Jews knew little of what occurred in the camps—drawn from her previous reading. But now she acquires new knowledge, cognitively dissonant from her current understanding—as Vladek asserts, "We knew the stories. . . . We knew everything" (*Maus I* 157). At this point, she can simply ignore the dissonance and not pursue a line of inquiry. Or she can work to understand the reasons for that dissonance. She opts for the latter: "Maybe it's because of Vladek's connections to the outside world that he was more aware of what was going on" (reading journal, April 2011). This seems a perfectly reasonable observation: being in the ghetto, Lewin would logically have little news of the outside world, especially during the chaotic days of the ghetto's liquidation, whereas Vladek has just now lost his freedom and his connection with the larger world.

We note, however, that Samantha does not fully consider the complexity of Vladek's perspective: Vladek tells his story from a vantage point constructed decades after the fact (in response to Art's queries). Samantha does not ask whether Vladek's memory has been distorted and shaped over time. Instead, she regards Vladek's account as contemporary with Lewin's—a misreading, although an understandable one. She does, however, come close to this realization when she observes the "differences in testimony": "Being exposed to different perspectives of the Shoah helps to 'decentralize' Shoah suffering and helps me try to view each Jew and survivor as their own individual, who experienced something unique and worthy of reflection in their own right" (reading journal, April 2011). Indeed, we suspect, having learned earlier of Samantha's respect for the "sanctity" of survivor testimony (and the inevitable "frailty of memory"), that she makes a conscious choice not to judge Vladek's account as flawed (Samantha, reading journal, March 2011). In that earlier commentary, she makes this unabashed declaration:

> It is painful to me to imagine the testimonies of people—human beings who *know*, like nobody else could ever even *imagine*, what it feels like to be engulfed with despair of the deepest sort, and to look out over their bit of Earth and see nothing—being disregarded as unreliable bits of "memory." Regardless of what any historian thinks, I believe there is something of intrinsic and intangible value in these accounts, and as a result I find myself (a lover of the power of truth and reality) reasoning that within memory, truth becomes relative. (Reading journal, March 2011)

We admire this response for its expression of feeling, of thoughtfulness, and level of comfort with seeming contradiction. "Without contraries is no progression," writes the poet William Blake, famously (7). We believe that Samantha's commentary embodies that truth. In the next and final chapter, we provide further evidence, at the course's end, of our students' complex and embodied learning.

7 ▪ Reclaiming Faith

Given the atrocities that Jews suffered during the Shoah because of their religion, a question of faith necessarily surfaced: How could one continue to believe in God?
Micah, "Jewish Faith and the Shoah," digital snapshot

In an age of testimony, and in view of contemporary history, I want my students to receive information that is *dissonant,* and not just congruent, with everything that they have learned beforehand.
Shoshana Felman, "Education and Crisis, or the Vicissitudes of Teaching"

Challenges to Faith

It has never been our intention to leave our students with dissonance only. It has never been our objective that students leave our course with faith shaken and certainties jettisoned. And yet as educators, and Shoah educators especially, we recognize the special power entrusted to us: the power to move students from "old" truths to "new" truths, from misconceptions to credible and substantiated belief. Yet even as we attempt to do so, the Shoah, as Micah suggests, represents a tremendous challenge, for those survivors who emerged from the Shoah and, we speculate, for those who regard the Shoah as a teaching subject. Is faith still possible after the Shoah? We might pose this question as well: Is teaching the Shoah possible? We ask the latter question not to engage the problem of representing an event that defies language or symbolic rendering. Rather we ask it because we speculate as to whether our students and ourselves can continue to believe in good and in right once we emerge from our studies of this tragic event.

When Rabbi Leo Baeck, the last "elected and appointed leader" of the Jewish community in Germany, emerged from the "model" concentration camp of Terezin or Theresienstadt, he retained his faith in the Jewish people and humankind. Despite the efforts of his captors to defeat him, he had survived intact. As his biographer writes, "He had lived through hell. He had not been broken. The community which he had led had died, but his task endured" (Friedlander, *Leo Baeck* 48). In the lead-up to the Shoah, Baeck helped to keep the Jewish community together and, when sent to Terezin, he did what he could to support those who, like himself, were trapped in that hellish environment. For the next decade he continued to teach and write, affirming the view that "teaching could surmount the nights of Terezin" (Friedlander, *Leo Baeck* 276).

Baeck's life and theology, which emphasized both the mystery of God and also the commandment to lead an ethical existence, demonstrate that the Shoah need not lead to cynicism or pessimism. For our students, and ourselves, the journey has not been an easy one. While we, of course, cannot directly experience the horrors of the Shoah, we are forced to confront it as honestly as we can. In this chapter we look at what our students take away from this encounter as reflected in their later journals, final examinations, and a sampling of their final projects. We hope to reflect also on what we, along with our students, derive from this arduous journey.

Confronting Challenges to Religious Faith

Early in the semester we ask students to engage this profound question: "Is faith possible after the Shoah?" We begin by looking at the experience of survivors themselves and to the work of theologians and philosophers who have undertaken the question. But we intend to include our students in this important conversation. In one of our readings, Steven T. Katz surveys the reactions of four theologians whose positions on the Shoah differ dramatically—from a rejection of the existence of God to an acceptance of the Shoah as "another cataclysmic event in Jewish history . . . , which calls on Jews to examine their consciences and learn lessons" (Mitchell and Mitchell, "The Holocaust and the Jewish Covenant" 411). This approach proves to be a challenge to our students, most of whom have some level of religious faith or at least faith in the goodness of humankind. The classic dilemma as to why God would allow such a thing to happen, known by its own subfield as theodicy, is front and center. Peter expresses this view: "For a person like myself who studies the Bible and has been tested throughout his life in extreme and tragic ways on several occasions . . . I'm always wondering why things happen the way they do" (reading journal, March 2011). Peter does not elaborate on his own experiences, but the events of the Shoah forces him to reflect on why "it was important for me to try to understand how the survivors of the Shoah may have felt."

Micah goes further in trying to come to terms with the challenge to religious faith when he reacts to the teaching of Jewish theologian Ignatz Maybaum. Micah selects the following passage to which to respond:

> Hitler was an instrument. . . . God used this instrument to cleanse, to purify, to punish a sinful world; the six million Jews, they died an innocent death; they died because of the sins of others. (Katz 420)

There could hardly be a more perplexing position to react to for our students, provocatively blaming the victims for their fate. However, Micah seizes on the passage as an opportunity:

> I was initially incredulous; never had I thought that I would read of a Jewish scholar describing this atrocity as a *churban,* an event signaling improvement. I questioned how anyone could even suggest redemption in the Holocaust. However, after reflecting on Maybaum's philosophy, I can see that it is not so absurd, that it is just a way to try to reconcile Jewish faith with the events of the Holocaust. (Reading journal, March 2011)

We note Micah's frankness here and his embrace of complex truths. It is one thing to acknowledge his initial incredulousness; it is another to think through a rationale for Maybaum's claim. To highlight the need to reconcile one's current faith with the reality of the Shoah seems an especially important realization.

Hillary, on the other hand, accepts the position of a theologian from the start, making exploration unnecessary. She is taken with Richard Rubenstein's view: "The Holocaust is proof that 'God is Dead'—if there were a God, He would surely have prevented Auschwitz. If He did not then He does not exist" (Katz 414). For many years, Hillary has held to the view that survivors were unlikely to believe in a god. Reading the Rubenstein article confirms what she thought to be true: "I am somewhat relieved to learn the truth" (reading journal, March 2011). She is less open than Micah to contrasting perspectives on this subject. For her the readings confirm what she felt she already knows.

From yet another perspective, Samantha is convinced by rabbinic scholar Elizear Berkovitz, who subscribes to the "notion of *hester panim* ('The hiding face of God')": "God's hiddenness brings into being the possibility for ethically valent human action, for by 'absenting' himself from history He creates the reality of human freedom which is necessary for moral behavior. . . . God has to abstain from reacting immediately to evil deeds if our action is to possess value" (Katz 422). Samantha comments,

> Berkovitz's views, in particular, demonstrated to me a very beau-
> tiful view of God and God's role in both history and Judaism. . . .
> The God Berkovitz sees is a god who truly has the human race's
> best interests "in mind," even if horrible things happen while he
> is away. (Reading journal, March 2011)

Samantha seems willing to accept a novel and positive view: that God can have humanity's back, as it were, while being invisible. She implies the novelty of such a view, given the "horrible things" that occurred during the Shoah. Prior to this reading, Samantha likely held the view that God could not be acting in humanity's interest in allowing tragic events to happen. In all these responses we observe students struggling to come to terms with what they have been reading and hearing of the horrors of the Shoah. Interestingly, all three have come to somewhat different conclusions on the question of religious faith. From a developmental point of view, this range of response is not unusual. Micah seems to be able to deal with uncertainty in the face of contrasting views, whereas Hillary, at least at this point, needs to know the "truth." Samantha appears to have come to a new perspective on the subject.

Unlearning and Re-Learning

After dealing with the horrors of the Shoah in the ghettos and camps, students encounter additional complexities, including a consideration of those who were not captured but still are traumatized by the Shoah (as in Appelfeld's novella *Tzili*) and the question, raised in Gross's *Neighbors,* of whether it "is possible to be simultaneously a victim and victimizer" (Gross 95). As Stefane notes in response to *Neighbors,* "By reading this work I have grasped a small portion of understanding when it came to Polish-Jewish relations in these events leading up to and during the Shoah, an understanding that was completely absent before the reading" (reading journal, 28 March 2011). In other words, Stefane is beginning to see the complex relationship between Polish Jews and their fellow citizens. Probing more deeply than Stefane, Michael adds this expanded understanding when reacting to the murders of the Jewish population by non-Jews in the Polish village of Jedwabne:

> The perpetrators were not Nazis; they were people who had been living besides these Jews all of their lives. Most of what we have read has been about the German's institutionalized maltreatment of the Jews, but this is as bad as what the Nazi were doing without the hand of the state guiding the actions of the perpetrators. (Reading journal, March 2011)

Michael's commentary serves as a welcome reminder to us as instructors: our emphasis on the Germans' systematized killing of millions perhaps leaves students with the impression that atrocities during the Shoah were committed by Germans alone. We would do well to qualify that assertion.

In our final examination we provide students with an additional opportunity to reflect on what they have learned by way of a reflective essay. As an option, students are given a prompt from Shoah scholar Lawrence Langer in which he observes, "Reading and writing about the Holocaust is an experience in *unlearning*" ("On Writing" 6). What did our students have to "unlearn"? What new learning took place? We thought that these were important questions, demonstrating how well our students have processed all that they have experienced during the semester. As we have come to see from their journals and class discussions, our students are capable of very thoughtful, and even profound, responses. We know that for many subjects, and especially one as complex as the Shoah, the act of unlearning is a prerequisite for greater understanding.

In his essay, Richard emphasizes the crucial point that "not only did I learn a tremendous amount about the Shoah, I learned it through unlearning." He writes, "If someone was to ask me what happened to the Jews between 1939–1945 I would have said 'they were put into cattle cars and sent to Auschwitz to die.' This class helped me unlearn that assumption, which at the time I thought was definite." He is then able to catalog the different points where his "unlearning" occurred:

> I was able to learn about the ghettos first through the words of Abraham Lewin, but then more vividly through Art Spiegelman's *Maus*. I was also able to learn that . . . some were murdered in their hometowns. . . . I learned that the Jews did not let their constant torture and dehumanization consume their lives, and instead took action by using various forms of resistance. (Final exam)

Richard's "unlearning" takes the form of not only learning about the existence of ghettos and resistance, but also coming to appreciate the difficulty of resisting both in the ghettos and the camps. As he reflects,

> I would have assumed it to be an easy decision to take up arms and fight the Nazis. Through this unlearning process I had realized that. . . . Jews had to calculate when and where they would fight. . . . But the more impossible fact to account for was that joining a partisan group, or conspiracy to escape, meant certain death to one's family. (Final exam)

Here Richard has come to understand not only the tremendous difficulty of finding arms and organizing, but also the moral dilemma of doing so and then putting one's family at almost certain risk of being executed.

In his assessment of his "unlearning," Richard, like most of our students, is particularly affected by Steven Ross, the survivor whom we had brought to our school. Ross's dramatic telling of his experiences has a tremendous impact on Richard: "[The presentation] truly showed me the power that deep memory holds" (final exam). The concept of "deep memory," which we had discussed earlier in the semester in connection with Charlotte Delbo's work, was concretized for Richard before his very eyes. A very important learning for him was "to let go of old assumptions," among them, it seems, the idea that trauma simply cannot be buried—it will come out (final exam). Perhaps most important for him was that "the Shoah cannot be explained in one paragraph, but needs to be told one story at a time" (final exam).

For Samantha, unlearning brings some uncertainty: "Although I came into this class with an open mind and a little bit of prior knowledge, it seemed the more I learned, the more questions (without answers) arose" (final exam). Here she hits on an important point we had tried to make in the course: that the Shoah raises more questions than answers. She seems to grasp this critical point when she writes, "It was difficult to reconcile my notions of humanity, history and truth with the material [that we] went over, but the unlearning that took place has only been beneficial, if not eye opening" (final exam). She particularly points to the importance of survivor testimony:

> The emphasis that this course placed on the human experience of the Shoah was something I was surprised by. . . . Survivor testimony helped me to give a face to the Shoah. . . . I had to unlearn that the term "survivor" only pertained to a literal Shoah survivor. . . . *Maus* 1 & 2 showed me that second generation survivors felt the impact of the Shoah as well. (final exam)

Samantha leaves the course with obviously expanded knowledge about the Shoah, but also with sincere questions about "what it means to be a good person . . . and my ideas about truth." She continues: "The more knowledge I came into, the more I wanted to know, the more questions I asked, and the more questions I asked the more distance any notion of truth or meaning became." She is perplexed by the existence of deniers "because after all of the works we read and the information we had ingested . . . here was this article [by Deborah Lipstadt] showing the insidious nature of people who knowingly disregard all that is known in favor of . . . false belief." As understandably disconcerting as this was for her and others, she leaves the course not dispirited, though, but rather with a "more acute and critical outlook" (final exam).

Hillary's "unlearning" process differs from Samantha's. For Hillary the key is connecting both the cognitive and affective response: "I 'learn' dates and facts, the dry, objective information, then I feel" (final exam). Hearing a survivor often brings the Shoah "home" for our students—makes it real—embodying both the details of the Shoah and the affective content. Hillary concurs:

> I had spent so many weeks formally learning about the details, even if through creative forms such as poetry and literature. When Steven Ross began speaking . . . I thought of Dan Pagis' poem "Written in Pencil" and the fear portrayed in the words. . . . In this moment, it was as real as it could ever be. (Final exam)

It may have taken Hillary longer than some others to make the connections between so-called "facts" and affect, but in the end she comes to this conclusion:

> Primary sources, secondary sources, spoken or written are all equally important . . . and when trying to "unlearn" [they] should all be present. . . . With the Shoah especially, knowing sometimes isn't enough.

Finally, on the subject of unlearning, Micah points to the fact that, like others, he "had some preconceived notions regarding the Shoah" that he needed to revisit (final exam). He particularly focuses on the question of the bystander:

> I had always accepted claims of powerlessness and ignorance by bystanders. However, after this [piece by Eric Sterling] and the other pieces we read, I had to unlearn this and reconsider."

He points to Neighbors, particularly, as requiring the most "unlearning":

> I had always assumed that the persecution of the Jews was carried out, or at least ordered, by the Nazis. . . . Seeing ordinary bystanders willingly kill their own Jewish neighbors, without direct involvement by the Germans, made me seriously recon-

sider my thoughts of mitigated bystander culpability. (Final exam)

In his discussion of *Neighbors,* however, Micah points to the complexity of this issue and perhaps the Shoah itself: "[M]any of the issues surrounding the Shoah are dealt with in shades of grey rather than with any definitive answers" (final exam). For Micah, and for others, this is an important lesson from the Shoah. Although we must make a clear demarcation between perpetrators and victims, we need also be mindful of what Primo Levi labels the "gray zone" (115).

Multiple, Digital Representations of the Shoah

In an effort to get our students to reflect further on the challenges of rendering the Shoah, we draw upon the critical social theorist Theodor Adorno, who famously argues that "to write poetry after Auschwitz is barbaric" (quoted in Hirsch and Kacandes 24). Such a view contradicts our stance in the course: that the subject can be rendered and done so in multiple modalities and genres, including poetry. While Andreea gives "credit to Adorno when he explains that the atrocities are unspeakable," she believes that poetry, in particular the work of Dan Pagis and Nelly Sach, gives voice to those who could not speak: "Sometimes, emotions are so unexplainable that putting words into poetry is the closest one can come to expressing their emotions. . . . [T]heir poetry gives us a small insight into the effects of the Shoah" (final exam). She believes also that Art Spiegelman's rendering of the Shoah in graphic form is important. "By choosing to write the story in graphic form he reached and bestowed knowledge upon others that might not have read it otherwise" (final exam). She defends in her essay Spiegelman's choice of the comic medium:

> [Spiegelman gave] a human condition to these people; we were able to fall in love when they did, and when they suffered we suffered with them. . . . In no way, shape or form did Spiegelman desecrate the Shoah. He did not victimize those who perished at the hands of the Nazis. Rather he honored them! (Final exam)

Finally Andreea discusses the importance of fiction when representing the Shoah. She observes the following in response to the short novel

Tzili: "For some, testimonies and historical accounts . . . are too much to bear. By fictionalizing stories . . . authors . . . reach out to those who might not have read other types of accounts" (final exam). Here Andreea passionately makes the case for multiple ways of representing the Shoah, a foundational assumption of this course since its inception.

The students featured come to understand what the historian Doris Bergen calls the "tension between the necessity of history and its inadequacy, between the expectations placed on it and the impossibility of meeting them" (38). To gain even a preliminary understanding of this complex event, the Shoah must be represented in multiple forms. Our course has attempted to do this through the variety of genres we have assigned (including music from the period) and the survivor testimony to which our students are exposed. In addition, we have for the last three years assigned as a final project a digital snapshot centering on a single point of inquiry. Although this can be a difficult assignment, our students have, for the most part, been able to rise to the challenge. The assignment allows for an intense exploration of a subject that students generate and find particularly interesting. The activity also promotes the digital representation of the Shoah in a format featuring multiple media.

The topics vary widely. Students express a desire to find something of redeeming value from this horrific narrative. For example, Michael and Andreea look at the effect on postwar medical ethics of the infamous "experiments" conducted by doctors in the camps (Michael, "In the Wake of the Angel of Death"; Andreea, "Medical Experiments in the Shoah"). Hillary explores the treatment of women and their resilience in the face of gender-specific discrimination ("Taking It All: Was Being a Female Prisoner a Unique Shoah Experience?"). Peter feels a need to explore why the United States did not do more to forestall the Shoah, and Jacob wants to understand the phenomenon of survivor guilt (Peter, "Could the United States Have Done More to Prevent the Shoah?"; Jacob, "What Role Did Feeling of Shared Guilt Have on the Lives of Holocaust Survivors?"). We are, on the whole, pleased with the results of our students' efforts and we offer four examples of their work, which serve as capstone projects for the course.

Stefane, investigating "The Lives of Perpetrators as Told through Images," designs a snapshot featuring photographs (some just recently discovered) of camp commandants, Gestapo, and police officials. These photographs portray SS officials assigned to Auschwitz enjoying a picnic as well as a "sing-along" by camp personnel outside the camp. Stefane also includes an excerpt from a diary of a Gestapo commander in which he describes his day-to-day duties of murder in detail, but with no remorse. She includes a quotation from the Shoah historian Christopher Browning: "mass murder and routine had become one" ("The Lives of Perpetrators"). For Stefane it was incomprehensible that people could be celebrating and living a "normal" life while committing such atrocities. It is, of course, one of the central dilemmas in studying the Shoah.

The photographs seen out of context could have been anywhere; people relaxing in lounge chairs or celebrating an annual holiday; the commander writing an impassioned love letter to a woman, but with no obvious feelings about the murder he was committing on a daily basis. Stefane, of course, could have no answer to the irony except to say that "to understand something you need to put reason to it, but there is no reason in genocide" ("The Lives of Perpetrators"). In fact, this seems a "reasonable" conclusion.

Richard's research efforts are no less reasonable as he explores "Rebellion through Unarmed Resistance": "In the face of constant degradation, humiliation, starvation, dehydration and other forms of torture, how did the Jewish people find a way to create forms of resistance?" Drawing on the vast resources of the United States Holocaust Memorial Museum and other sources, his snapshot reflects the many forms of resistance in the ghettos and camps. These include a picture of a resistance group in the Minsk Ghetto and examples of the varieties of resistance, including spiritual and cultural. The ghettos formed underground newspapers and radio, schools, and a variety of cultural and religious activities. Individuals served as couriers to the outside world, and there were special roles for women and children. Although resistance was understandably difficult in the camps, Richard portrays the ways that Jews, for example, prayed together and used whatever materials they could to commemorate Jewish holidays—a form of cultural and spiritual resistance.

Students such as Richard need a sense that something more came out of the Shoah than the horror. As he points out in an interview, "I did my project on it because, for one thing, I wanted something uplifting—beyond atrocities. . . . I had never thought about the idea of resistance and rescue." Researching and examining the many ways that Jews in the ghettos and in the camps were able to resist their captors provide him (and us) with the sense that they were not one-dimensional victims going to their deaths without a struggle. Richard's project portrays those victimized during the Shoah as individuals who struggled as best they could to survive and to resist. For Richard and others in the class, this is part of the process of both learning and unlearning.

Focusing not on resistance but on art as a tool for survival, Samantha, whose project is titled "The Role of Art: How Does Art Help Shoah Survivors Cope with Their Experiences?" writes, "Shoah art is a preservation memory, of experience, and all of time itself. The result of the creative catharsis of artists connected to the Shoah is the representation of a point of time without a counterpart." Prominent in her piece is a painting by David Olère representing "a Jewish family arriving at a camp and on the verge of death." She is able to perceive the artist's irony, noting the double nature of the "spectral, emaciated ghost hovering above" the family, signaling their "imminent death," while observing the ghost's "protective gesture" predicting the end of their torments. She also includes a painting by Shoah survivor and artist Samuel Bak, *Sounds of Silence,* in which "blind musicians play on broken instruments with prosthetic limbs and shadowy bodies [with sheet music] left blank." She correctly concludes that, for Bak, the Shoah resists the musician's effort to render the pain and suffering incurred.

These digital snapshots provide students with an opportunity to return to a topic that captured their interest earlier in the semester. That certainly is the case with Micah, who continues his exploration of faith and the Shoah, about which he reflects in his journal. In a most impressive and thorough snapshot titled, "Jewish Faith in the Shoah," Micah explores three main schools of post-Shoah Jewish faith: the Shoah within the context of traditional Judaism, the Shoah as inexplicable, and the absence of God after the Shoah. Micah briefly discusses leading theologians whose writings reflect one of these positions, as well as the writer Elie Wiesel, who, in his iconic *Night,* chronicles the severe challenge to faith posed by the experience of Auschwitz. The snapshot also includes video featuring a survivor who has renounced his faith. Micah does not take a stand on this controversial question. Rather, he concludes by writing that "years later questions of faith in relation to the Shoah remain a prominent feature of modern Jewish life" ("Jewish Faith and the Shoah"). Micah, like many of the students in the class, has discovered that the study of the Shoah leaves us with more questions than answers. Being able to tolerate such ambiguity is itself an important lesson.

Our Own Unlearning:
Implications for Teaching and Research

When we undertook to design a course about the Shoah, we felt, frankly, like the novices that we were. After all, neither of us had been trained in Shoah studies. We entered the class on that first day knowing precious little, clinging precariously to the texts that we had assigned. But there we were: teaching a course that neither of us had expected to teach—a course that, as we note earlier, we had studiously avoided teaching. Among aspects of this course that required "unlearning" must surely have been an evolving and flexible notion of expertise, especially at a teaching institution such as a public community college. Upon what authority can any of us claim to teach our courses? Our credentials in the form of graduate degrees make one kind of argument for our presence in front of the classroom. But credentialing speaks of the work that we had done at the point of hire and not the hard work of continuing to deepen that expertise. If there is one thing we have learned about the teaching profession it is that unless we commit ourselves to learning on the job—expanding our expertise— we cease to be effective practitioners. Expertise boasts a dynamic quality; remaining static, it should lose its value and the authority which it confers. Our needing to "cultivate" our understanding of the Shoah in literature and history continues to serve as a catalyst for our own learning about the subject of the Shoah and about best teaching practices. This book is, in part, an effort to demonstrate that journey.

Against the backdrop of a community college in which teaching loads can be crushing, we make the argument with some urgency: that unless we remain intellectually curious, engage in classroom research, and seek to experiment with course design (and redesign), we run the risk of stagnating and, worse, ceasing to care about the work and our students' chances for success. We recognize the limits of our argument: where is the time to become truly an expert in the Shoah? Yet the expertise to which we refer consists less of mastery of the subject and more of a readiness to observe, to reflect on, and to write about the teaching of that subject.

These two broad notions—that expertise should be dynamic rather than static and that research becomes the fuel to nurture that dynamism—are hardly unique to our course or to our institution but, rather, can be applied across subject areas and institutions. We also offer some narrower, but no less significant, lessons gained from our experience, lessons in unlearning, that we trust can be useful to others:

Render disciplinary methods and habits of mind explicit

- The longer we teach, the less aware we become of the various assumptions and methods that characterize our disciplines. These ways of knowing and doing business have become, indeed, habits. They have become part of us. We may grant that virtually all of our students enter our class in order to gain content knowledge and give little, if any, regard to disciplinary knowledge. But if we are serious about the business of transfer, of giving students the skills and knowledge sets that they can deploy in a variety of settings and situations, we need to bring to their attention what will transfer.

Model such methods and habits

- "Walking the walk" is very important. In other words, we do our students a service if we can demonstrate by our actions the ways of thinking and problem posing that help define our disciplines. All teachers know the value of modeling for students, but such modeling requires that we be aware of our own practices in the classroom and that we at times take the risk of showing what it means to address problems and questions without clear and unambiguous answers. In the 1990s, Gerald Graff urged us to "teach the conflicts"—advice that still resonates. Let us not be afraid to tell our students that differences of opinion exist on an issue. Experts can disagree, and with good reason.

Encourage students to transfer those methods and habits to new domains and situations
- A course about the Shoah has, we believe, a moral imperative of transfer. We hope that students will apply what they have learned to settings and scenes beyond the classroom, most notably through intervention when intolerance is displayed. But we wish to encourage transfer in its strict sense: the application of defined skills and knowledge sets to new situations. We would expect, for example, that students deploy the historian's reverence for nuanced causation—seeking multiple and various causes rather than reducing an event to one simple cause. And we would hope to see students display an awareness of the rhetorical situation, including the need to understand the imperatives of genre and of audience. More profoundly, we look to our students to leave our course with a readiness to reflect and an ability to "think about thinking" (Berthoff).

Create opportunities for integrative learning
- Perhaps of all the lessons that we have learned and continue to learn from this course, promoting true, integrative learning may be the most challenging to implement. We have documented our struggles to break down the barriers of our disciplines so as to give our students a holistic and integrative experience. Such is not easy if we have been thoroughly trained and if we value the discipline-specific qualities of our work. Moreover, we realize that institutions are still defined by and large by departments and specialties. Still, the payoff is rich indeed if we create space in our

courses for a kind of splicing of disciplines. Assigning complex works that blur the lines between disciplines and genres is an important first step. For us, Jan Gross's *Neighbors* and Art Spiegelman's *Maus* serve that purpose. History, sociology, politics, ethnography, and historiography converge in Gross's book. In *Maus* we witness the convergence not only of word and image but a "comix"ture of genres—from the memoir to the map, from broad historical narrative to family album. It makes sense for us, then, to ask students to report on a research question that crosses disciplinary boundaries and to do so in a format that is digital and multimodal. We encourage colleagues to use web tools and the digital environment in order to create opportunities for integrative learning.

Foster both the affective and critical response

- A course on the Shoah engages the hearts of students and the faculty who instruct them. At first we first found this fact troubling. Given our personal connection to the subject and the traumatic content of the course, we feared that we and our students would lose objectivity and become too involved and risk exposure (a taboo in academia). That remains a concern, to be sure, but now we realize the benefits of "whole response." If readings produce a deeply emotional response, then as instructors we need to provide a space for that response to be expressed. Hence, we allow for a frank reaction in weekly reading journals, as well as time within the classroom (and in our offices) for "debriefing." But we want students to be able to step back from their readings and to adopt a critical stance. The question "How does this reading broaden your understanding of the Shoah?" greets students at the end of each journal, with the purpose of promoting a wider, somewhat comprehensive and critical reaction to the reading. Carefully calibrated questions, within the safe environment of small groups, help bring about a synthesis of the affective and cognitive or critical. In their final research projects, students must "own" their research question—that means they must bring their hearts and minds to the task of posing and probing that question. We appreciate that given a diverse student body, those who come into our class may be at different developmental levels. We hope that the challenge of the course and the scaffolding we have built will help them to further those qualities that they will need as they move forward on their academic journeys.

Teach (and write) with colleagues outside your discipline and area of expertise

- In graduate school—at least in the humanities—we are essentially told that as teachers and publishing scholars we will be working alone. The classroom is ours to do with as we wish, the work of research is "our time" to work on our own without interruption, and the publications that we submit must bear only our name (and, of course, "peer reviewed" only at the end of the process). Those had been our own expectations until we began to teach and write together. Our collaboration has not been easy, since each of us is a product of conventional graduate training in which the paradigm of solitary scholarship prevailed. Moreover, as teachers we share the performance anxiety of all classroom practitioners, from preschool through graduate school. But we have come to be more comfortable teaching in front of the other and, with that increased comfort and the validation provided by a colleague in the same room, each of us has become more confident as teachers. We have also been blessed from time to time to have other colleagues from a variety of disciplines sit in on our class, and their feedback has been invaluable.

Our different disciplinary practices are laid bare in our classroom behavior, syllabus design, and textbook assignment, and call out for our understanding—individually and jointly. Our collaboration does not end with the classroom, as we have written and presented conference papers together and jointly written this book. Even as we write this last chapter (via a wiki), we engage in e-mail conversation about our different ways of rendering classroom experience:

> Howard: Again, we're being descriptive and not analytical, Ron. Shouldn't we comment on [the] meaning [of the student's observations]?
>
> Ron: Howard, I guess this is where the difference sometimes lies between history, which tends to be more descriptive, and lit, which is analytic. (Tinberg and Weisberger)

Whereas one of us seems more comfortable with providing a narrative of our course, the other seems to prefer analysis; one favors chronological rendering of classroom experience, and the other foregrounds the thematic; one relies on the past tense when chronicling the story of this class, and the other sees virtue in the immediate present. And so we continue to struggle, inhabiting the other person's perspective as best we can. This book, we believe, offers testimony (a key term in Shoah studies) as to how far we, and our students, have traveled.

APPENDIX A. COURSE SYLLABUS

ENG 264

Remembering the Holocaust in Literature and History: An Honors Interdisciplinary Seminar

Mondays, 4:00–6:40 PM

Web Page: contentbuilder.merlot.org/toolkit/users/HT/bcceng64

Contact Info:

Howard Tinberg

Office Hours: M–W 12:30–1:45 PM (or by appointment)

Office: B215

Phone: 678-2811, ext. 2317

E-mail: Howard.Tinberg@bristolcc.edu

Ron Weisberger

Office Hours: M–F 9:00–5:00 (by appointment)

Office: B-110a

Phone: 678-2811, ext. 2444

E-mail: Ron.Weisberger@bristolcc.edu

What is this course about?

The Holocaust, or, as it has come to be known, the Shoah, is one of the most horrific events in all of world history. Even more than fifty years after the fact, the world continues to struggle with the enormity of this human catastrophe. Nevertheless, a body of writing—both historical and literary—exists that enables us to confront this key moment in world history. This course serves as an introduction to this work. Students gain an understanding of the historical facts, including circumstances leading up to the Holocaust itself and the event's critical aftermath. In addition, students reflect on the role of literature, principally through accounts of that time written by survivors and the

children of survivors, in the struggle to represent an event that many have described as beyond the limits of language to capture.
Prerequisite: ENG 101 and ENG 102. Open to Commonwealth Honors Program students and others with permission of instructors.

Is there a web component for this course?
Yes. This course has a home page (see above), on which reading and writing assignments are posted.

What reading is expected?
We will be using a variety of texts this semester: a collection of historically based readings, a case study of a particular town in Poland during the Holocaust, an anthology of Holocaust literature, a graphic novel (in two parts), and survivor testimony. Reading assignments are given below. Please read each weekly assignment prior to that week's class. Supplemental works are given on the course website or, as in the case of videos, will be shown in class.

What writing will I be expected to do?
You will be expected to keep a typed reading journal, an entry due in class each week. In addition, you will have a midterm and final exam and a semester-culminating research project.

What is plagiarism? What are its consequences?
We expect that your writing will be your own. If you draw upon the work of others, we expect that you acknowledge that work appropriately. If you do not do so, serious consequences are likely to follow, including a dramatic reduction of your grade on a particular assignment.

What penalties do I incur when work is handed in late?
All deadlines need to be respected. A reduction of a half-grade will be exacted for every day an assignment (draft or journal) is late.

May I use a cell phone and laptop computer during class?

While we appreciate the need to keep in touch with friends and family in case of an emergency, we are asking that you set your cell phones on silent during class and refrain from texting. Laptops need to be turned off and closed up during class, unless we've indicated otherwise.

What is the relative weight of each assignment?

Your research project will count for 35 percent of your course grade. Your midterm and final will each count for a quarter of your grade. Your reading journal work will count 15 percent. Here is the breakdown:

Midterm	25%
Final	25%
Reading Journal	15%
Research Project	35%

When (and how) can I withdraw from this course without penalty?

The last day on which you can officially withdraw is Wednesday, April 11. To do so, you will need to contact the records office in G building (second floor). The folks there will give you the proper paperwork. If you need to withdraw after that date, please talk or write to us, and we'd be glad to withdraw you. If you withdraw without informing us, however, the penalty is severe: you will be given a grade for the course that will include a mark for the work that you've missed.

How many absences am I allowed?

Attendance is required. If you miss more than six hours of class (two class sessions), and do not officially withdraw from this course, you run the risk of suffering at least a full-grade reduction.

Where can I go for additional help?

For academic support, you may want to consult a tutor at the Tutoring and Academic Support Center (TASC) in B-110. The TASC is open 8:00 AM–8:00 PM Monday–Thursday, 8:00 AM–5:00 PM Friday, and 9:00 AM–12:00 PM, Saturday. For information call ext. 2295.

We suggest that you try the Writing Center in B117 at ext. 2544 (please call or visit to find out the Center's hours). The Writing Center offers free tutoring for the writing that you do in this or any course. Staffed by student and faculty tutors, the center provides a supportive environment in which to work on your writing. We urge you to visit.

Bristol Community College complies with federal legislation for individuals with disabilities (Section 504 of the Rehabilitation Act of 1973 and the Americans with Disabilities Act of 1990 and the ADAA of 2009) and offers reasonable accommodations to qualified students with disabilities. It is your responsibility to notify the Office of Disability Services of your need for classroom accommodations. Accommodations are arranged through the Office of Disability Services/ODS, which will issue a confidential Disability Services Accommodation Form. This should be accomplished, when possible, during the first two weeks of class. If you have questions about the process, please contact ODS by calling (508) 678-2811, ext. 2955, or stop by B104. You may also contact ODS online at www.bristol.mass.edu/Students/ods/request_forms/ods_contact_us.cfm

What books will I need to purchase?
Here are the required texts for the course:

Art from the Ashes: A Holocaust Anthology. Ed. Lawrence L. Langer. New York: Oxford UP, 1995. ISBN 0-19-507559-5
Gross, Jan T. *Neighbors.* New York: Penguin, 2002. ISBN 0-691-08667-2
Mitchell, Joseph R., and Helen Buss Mitchell, ed. *The Holocaust: Readings & Interpretations.* New York: McGraw-Hill/Dushkin, 2001. ISBN 0-07-244816-4
Spiegelman, Art. *Maus I: My Father Bleeds History.* New York: Pantheon, 1986. ISBN 0-394-74723-2
———. *Maus II: And Here My Troubles Began.* New York: Pantheon: 1991. ISBN 0-679-72977-1

What Holocaust-related sites on the World Wide Web do you recommend?
Several links to valuable Holocaust-related websites are available on our course website.

READINGS and TOPICS for DISCUSSION
Week of January 30
Introduction
>   The Structure of this Course: An Overview
>   The Reading Journal
>   Defining Terms
>   The Roots of Prejudice

Week of February 6
The Way It Was
>   Isaac Bashevis Singer, "The Spinoza of Market Street" (web link)
>   In-Class Workshop on Designing a Web Snapshot

Week of February 13
The Way It Was (cont.)
>   Rita Steinhardt Botwinick, "The Nazi Rise to Power" (Mitchell and Mitchell 63–76)
>   Klaus P. Fischer, "German and Jew in the Weimar Period" (Mitchell and Mitchell 78–86)

Week of February 20
Monday is Presidents' Day
Tuesday becomes a Monday
The Deportations and Ghettos
>   Ida Fink, "The Key Game" and "A Spring Morning" (*Art from the Ashes*, 241–48)
>   Abraham Lewin, "Diary of the Great Deportation" (*Art from the Ashes* 159–96)

Week of February 27
Gender and the Shoah
>   Myrna Goldenberg, "'From a World Beyond': Women in the Holocaust" (Mitchell and Mitchell 365–75)
>   Charlotte Delbo, "Voices" (*Art from the Ashes* 75–92)

Week of March 5
Midterm
History and Memory I
James E. Young, "Between History and Memory: The Uncanny Voices of Historian and Survivor" (Mitchell and Mitchell 532–41)

Week of March 12
Break

Week of March 19
The Shoah and the Art of Fiction
Aharon Appelfeld, *Tzili* (*Art from the Ashes* 271–341)

Week of March 26
Reclaiming Faith after the Shoah
Genesis 4:1–16
Job
Dan Pagis [all the poems] (*Art from the Ashes,* 584–97)
Steven T. Katz, "Jewish Faith after the Holocaust: Four Approaches" (Mitchell and Mitchell 410–23)

Week of April 2
History and Memory II
Jan Gross, *Neighbors*
Slawomir Grunberg, *The Legacy of Jedwabne* (film)

Week of April 9
Resistance and Rescue
Yehuda Bauer, "Forms of Jewish Resistance During the Holocaust" (Mitchell and Mitchell 256–62)
Nechama Tek, "From Self-Preservation to Rescue" (Mitchell and Mitchell 278–85)

Week of April 16
Monday is Patriots Day
Thursday becomes a Monday
Bystanders
    James Carroll, "The Holocaust and the Catholic Church" (Mitchell and Mitchell 304–10)
    Eric Sterling, "Indifferent Accomplices" (Mitchell and Mitchell 183–92)

Week of April 23
Nuremberg Trials
    Howard Ball, "World War II in Europe and the Nuremberg Tribunal" (Mitchell and Mitchell 450–61)

Week of April 30
The Second Generation
    Art Spiegelman, *Maus I* and *II*

Week of May 7
Presentations of Research
Review for Final Exam

Week of May 14
Final Exam

APPENDIX B. READING JOURNAL TEMPLATE

Reading Journal

We would like you to keep a reading journal for this course, in order to have you engage actively in what you read. Please keep this form when writing up your responses to the readings. Keep in mind that, when grading the journal, we will be considering the following:

- Appropriateness to the question
- Relevance and precision of detail from the reading
- Fullness of your response
- Depth of insights

Total points possible: 20

Your writing may be informal—you are not writing an essay. But we are requiring you to type your journal. Please aim for at least a full-page, single-spaced journal entry, in 11- or 12-point type.

Journals are due in class each week. Penalties apply for late journals.

Name: _____
Date: _____
Title of Reading: _____

1. Please quote a passage from the assigned readings for the week that resonates with you (captures your attention), giving the appropriate page reference.
2. We are interested in your reaction(s) to the passage. Questions you might consider as you reflect on the passage include Why did you choose this particular one? How did it enhance your understanding of the topic for the week? How did it further your understanding of the Shoah as a whole? How did it make you feel? Did the passage reinforce or change your mind about any aspect of the subject? Feel free to express yourself as best you can, taking into consideration the criteria mentioned above.

APPENDIX C. CRITICAL RESEARCH PROJECT

The Assignment

This assignment asks that you develop a thoughtful and significant question about the Shoah, state a thesis in response to that question, and, through careful research, provide relevant evidence in support of your thesis. You will not present your work in a conventional paper, however, but through a visual (and, potentially, auditory) medium in the form of a web "snapshot." A web snapshot might be seen as a digital or electronic poster. Instead of a paper poster board, you are creating a web page that can provide not only words, but also photos and other graphics, sound, and video. In addition, you will be asked to give an oral presentation at our last class, a presentation that will not summarize your snapshot but will rather address questions about the process that you went through in doing the research (see below). You will be given a guide on how to set up a snapshot. Further assistance will be provided, as needed.

Possible Subjects:
- Faith after Auschwitz
- Resistance to the Nazi regime
- American response to the Shoah
- Apportioning guilt for bystanders
- Motivation of rescuers
- Nazi oppression of the disabled
- Survivor guilt
- Legacy of the Shoah on children of survivors
- Function and outcome of the Nuremberg Trials
- Women and the Shoah
- Shoah Art
- Shoah monuments

Required Components of Snapshot

Your snapshot should include the following:

- A clear statement of a problem or research question (for example, How did "ordinary" Germans reconcile their destructive acts with the banality of their everyday routines?)

- A thesis in response to that question (for example, "Ordinary" Germans managed to live a kind of double life in order to achieve such reconciliation)

- Evidence in support of that thesis, properly acknowledged and cited in Modern Language Association (MLA) or American Psychological Association (APA) format

- An annotated bibliography (in MLA or APA format) summarizing and evaluating a minimum of six sources:

    1. One should be a primary source (for example: survivor testimony, a diary written at the time or a photograph taken at the time or a memoir written after the fact but by an eyewitness)
    2. Three must be scholarly sources (written by an expert—an article in a peer-reviewed journal or a scholarly book)
    3. Two must be drawn from our course readings (in addition to the sources as required in #1 and #2, above).

Please take care to observe copyright laws. Remember that a web page is NOT a paper. We expect that you will provide evidence of your research in a fashion appropriate to the digital medium.

Required Components of Oral Presentation

We ask that you present your project to your classmates and to others at the very end of the semester. Your oral presentation, which should run between five and ten minutes, will require you to answer the following questions:

- What question did you seek to answer?
- Why did you choose this question?
- What assumptions did you have about your subject when starting out?
- What surprised you, if anything, in the process of researching your question?

Evaluating Your Web Snapshot and Oral Presentation

Here is the breakdown of points for each part of your project:

Web Snapshot   20 points
Oral Presentation   5 points

We will evaluate your snapshots on the basis of the following criteria:

Research Subject (5 points)
- Clarity/focus
- Significance

Evidence (5 points)
- Relevance
- Credibility
- Documentation in MLA or APA style

Visual and Auditory Appeal (5 points)
- Balance of image and word and sound
- Purposeful use of fonts, colors, images
- Neatness

Language (5 points)
- Clarity
- Ownership
- Grammar and mechanics

Total: 20 points

We will evaluate your oral presentation on the basis of the following criteria (partial credit for each item is possible):

- Addressing the required questions (1 point)
- Appropriateness of your response (1 point)
- Clarity of your response (1 point)
- Meeting the time requirement (1 point)
- Displaying your snapshot (1 point)

Total: 5 points

Important Dates

In-Class Workshop on Designing a Web Snapshot	Feb. 6
Title and Research Question	Feb. 27
List of Sources in Modern Languages Association (MLA) or American Psychological Association (APA) format	March 26
Draft Web Snapshot (via email to Howard.Tinberg@bristolcc.edu and Ronald.Weisberger@bristolcc.edu)	April 9
Final Snapshot Links via E-mail to Howard.Tinberg@bristolcc.edu and Ronald.Weisberger@bristolcc.edu by start of class	May 7
Oral Presentations in Class	May 7

Late penalties apply for work handed in after deadline and will be deducted in evaluating your final project.

Midterm Exam Essay Prompt:
III. Essay (50 points). Choose ONE.

A.

"The origins of humiliation," writes Lawrence Langer in reference to survivors' accounts, "were often dissimilar for men and women, because womanhood and manhood were threatened in various ways. But the ultimate sense of loss unites former victims in a violated world beyond gender." In a clear and thoughtful essay, offer your thoughts on the role of gender in Shoah testimony. Please refer in detail to at least TWO of the works that we have read so far, one being our history text and the other drawn from the literature. You may, in addition, make use of the testimony that we have heard.

B.

The study of the Shoah, some have argued, begins at the intersection of memory and historical documentation. In other words, what we know of the Shoah is the product both of human memory and the historical record left by perpetrators and victims. In a clear and thoughtful essay, write about the contribution that each—memory and the historical record—plays. We suggest that you begin with definitions: What is memory? What is fact? In the study of the Shoah, where do the two converge? Where do they diverge or differ? Then proceed to compose an essay that refers in detail to at least TWO of the works that we have read so far, one being our history text and the other drawn from the literature. You may, in addition, make use of the testimony that we have heard.

Final Exam Essay Prompt:
IV. Essay (50 points). Choose ONE.

A.

The historian Rita Botwinick has observed, "One can merely say that neither the tormented or their tormentors ever received their full measure of justice." Drawing upon Shoah history, literature, and testimony, write a clear and thoughtful essay on (a) what you think Botwinick means and (b) whether or not you agree with her statement. Please provide detailed, relevant and appropriate evidence to support your claim. Although the emphasis is on the works that we have read in the second half of the course, feel free to draw on any of the assigned texts.

B.

"Reading and writing about the Holocaust is an experience in *unlearning*," observes the scholar Lawrence Langer. What do you think Langer means by that statement? What detailed, relevant, and appropriate evidence can you provide from your reading this semester, including history, literature, and testimony? In a clear and thoughtful essay, offer your thoughts on the *"unlearning"* that, according to Langer, inevitably takes place when reading and writing about the *Shoah*. What did you have to *unlearn*? What new learning replaced your old thinking on the subject? Although the emphasis is on the works that we have read in the second half of the course, feel free to draw on any of the assigned texts.

C.

Sociologist and philosopher Theodor Adorno once famously observed that "to write poetry after Auschwitz is barbaric." Adorno believed that, given the "unspeakable" atrocities that occurred during the Shoah, any attempt to represent the Shoah in words or images, no matter the writer's intention, will merely add to the desecration of the subject and further victimize those who perished at the hands of the Nazis. In the end, Adorno believed, the Shoah transcends art. What is your view of the matter? In a clear and thoughtful essay that draws in detail upon history, literature, and testimony, examine the Shoah as an "unspeakable" subject, beyond language and beyond image: Is art possible after Auschwitz? Although the emphasis is on the works that we have read in the second half of the course, feel free to draw on any of the assigned texts.

WORKS CITED

Abzug, Robert H. "Epilogue: The Changing Historical Perspective." *America Views the Holocaust, 1933–1945: A Brief Documentary History*. Ed. Robert H. Abzug. Boston: Bedford/St. Martin's, 1999. 207–13. Print.

"An accordionist leads a sing-along for SS officers." *Photo Archives*. U.S. Holocaust Memorial Museum, n.d. Web. 15 Aug. 2012.

Appelfeld, Aharon. *Tzili*. *Art from the Ashes: A Holocaust Anthology*. Ed. Lawrence Langer. New York: Oxford UP, 1995. 273–341. Print.

Arendt, Hannah. *Eichmann in Jerusalem: A Report on the Banality of Evil*. New York: Viking, 1963. Print.

Association of American Colleges and Universities. *Greater Expectations: A New Vision for Learning as a Nation Goes to College*. Association of American Colleges and Universities. 2002. Web. 21 June 2012.

Bak, Samuel. *Sounds of Silence*. *Samuel Bak—Gallery 3*. University of Minnesota Center for Holocaust and Genocide Studies. Web. 5 Apr. 2013.

Bartrop, Paul R. "A Little More Understanding: The Experience of a Holocaust Educator in Australia." *Teaching about the Holocaust: Essays by College and University Teachers*. Ed. Samuel Totten, Paul R. Bartrop, and Steven Leonard Jacobs. Westport, CT: Prager, 2004. N.pag. Kindle.

Bartov, Omer. "Testimonies as Historical Evidence: Reconstructing the Holocaust From Below." University of Minnesota Center for Holocaust and Genocide Studies, n.d. Web. 16 Aug. 2012.

Bass, Randy. "The Scholarship of Teaching: What's the Problem?" *Inventio* 1.1 (1999): n. pag. Web. 21 July 2011.

Bauer, Yehuda. *American Jewry and the Holocaust: The American Jewish Joint Distribution Committee, 1939–1945*. Detroit, MI: Wayne State University Press, 1981. Print.

———. "Is the Holocaust Explicable?" *The Holocaust: Readings and Interpretations*. Ed. Joseph R. Mitchell and Helen Buss Mitchell. New York: McGraw-Hill/ Dushkin, 2001. 19–31. Print.

Baxter-Magolda, Marcia. *Knowing and Reasoning in College: Gender-Related Patterns in Students' Intellectual Development*. San Francisco: Jossey-Bass, 1991. Print.

Belenky, Mary Field, Blyther McVicker Clinchy, Nancy Rule Goldberger, and Jill Mattuck Tarule. *Women's Ways of Knowing: The Development of Self Voice and Mind*. 10th anniversary ed. New York: Basic, 1997. Print.

Bergen, Doris L. "The Barbarity of Footnotes: History and the Holocaust." *Teaching the Representation of the Holocaust*. Ed. Marianne Hirsch and Irene Kacandes. New York: Modern Language Association. 2004. Print.

Bernard-Donals, Michael. *An Introduction to Holocaust Studies*. Upper Saddle River, NJ: Pearson, 2006. Print.

Berthoff, Ann E. *Forming, Thinking, Writing: The Composing Imagination*. Rochelle Park, NJ: Hayden, 1978.

Blake, William. "Marriage of Heaven and Hell." *The William Blake Archive*. Lib. of Cong., 2012. Web. 31 July 2012.

Botwinick, Rita Steinhardt. *A History of the Holocaust*. 4th ed. Boston: Prentice Hall, 2010.

———. "The Nazi Rise to Power." *The Holocaust: Readings and Interpretations*. Ed. Joseph R. Mitchell and Helen Buss Mitchell. New York: McGraw-Hill/ Dushkin, 2001. 63–76. Print.

Boyer, Ernest L. *College: The Undergraduate Experience*. New York: Harper Collins, 1987. Print.

———. *Scholarship Reconsidered: Priorities of the Professorate*. San Francisco: Jossey-Bass, 1990. Print.

Brandt, Deborah. *Literacy in American Lives*. Cambridge: Cambridge UP, 2001. Print.

Bristol Community College. *Fact Sheet Fall 2010*. 2012. Print.

———. *Fifth-Year Report*. Bristol Community College, 2009. Web. 27 Aug. 2012.

Britton, James. *The Development of Writing Abilities (11–18)*. London: Macmillan, 1975. Print.

Browning, Christopher R. *Ordinary Men: Reserve Police Battalion 101 and the Final Solution in Poland*. New York: Harper, 1993. Print.

Carroll, James. "The Holocaust and the Catholic Church." *The Holocaust: Readings and Interpretations*. Ed. Joseph R. Mitchell and Helen Buss Mitchell. New York: McGraw-Hill/Dushkin, 2001. 304–10. Print.

Cassedy, Ellen. *We Are Here: Memories of the Lithuanian Holocaust*. Lincoln: U of Nebraska P, 2012. Print.

Chiseri-Strater, Elizabeth. "Turning In upon Ourselves: Positionality, Subjectivity, and Reflexivity in Case Study and Ethnographic Research." *Ethics and Representation in Qualitative Studies of Literacy*. Ed. Peter Mortensen and Gesa E. Kirsch. Urbana, IL: National Council of Teachers of English. 115–33. Print.

Cushman, Ellen. *The Struggle and the Tools: Oral and Literate Strategies in an Inner City Community*. Albany: State U of New York P, 1998. Print.

Dean, Carolyn J. *The Fragility of Empathy after the Holocaust*. Ithaca, NY: Cornell UP, 2004. Print.

Delbo, Charlotte. "Voices." *Art from the Ashes: A Holocaust Anthology*. Ed. Lawrence Langer. New York: Oxford UP, 1995. 77–92. Print.

Dershowitz, Alan. *Chutzpah*.New York: Touchstone, 1992. Print.

Emig, Janet. *The Composing Processes of Twelfth Graders*. Urbana, IL: National Council of Teachers of English, 1971. Print.

Engel, David. *The Holocaust: The Third Reich and the Jews*. Essex, UK: Longman, 2000. Print.

Engstrom, Cathy, and Vincent Tinto. "Access without Support Is Not Opportunity." *Change* 40.1 (2008): 46–50. Print.

Epstein, Helen. *Children of the Holocaust: Conversations with Sons and Daughters of Survivors*. New York: Penguin, 1979. Print.

Erikson, Erik. *Identity: Youth and Crisis*. New York: Norton, 1968. Print.

Exposing the Holocaust Hoax Archive, n.d. Web. 9 Aug. 2012.

Feinstein, Stephen C. "What are the Results? Reflections on Working in Holocaust Education." *Teaching about the Holocaust: Essays by College and University*

Teachers. Ed. Samuel Totten, Paul R. Bartrop, and Steven Leonard Jacobs. Westport, CT: Praeger, 2004. Kindle.

Felman, Shoshana. "Education and Crisis, or the Vicissitudes of Teaching." *Testimony: Crises of Witnessing in Literature, Psychoanalysis, and History.* Ed. Shoshana Felman and Dori Laub. New York: Routledge, 1992. 1–56. Print.

Fink, Ida. "The Key Game." *Art from the Ashes: A Holocaust Anthology.* Ed. Lawrence Langer. New York: Oxford UP, 1995. 242–43. Print.

———. "A Spring Morning." In *Art from the Ashes: A Holocaust Anthology.* Ed. Lawrence Langer. New York: Oxford UP, 1995. 244–48. Print.

"Flossenburg." *United States Holocaust Memorial Museum.* U.S. Holocaust Memorial Museum, 2012. Web. 11 July 2012.

Friedlander, Albert H. *Leo Baeck: Teacher of Theresienstadt.* Woodstock, NY: Overlook P, 1991. Print.

———, ed. *Out of the Whirlwind: A Reader of Holocaust Literature.* Rev. ed. New York: UAHC P, 1999. Print.

Gabb, Sally, Howard Tinberg, and Ron Weisberger. "Kegan's Theory of Development Applied to Community College Students." *The Oxford University Handbook of Lifelong Learning.* Ed. Manuel London. New York: Oxford UP, 2011. 102–16. Print.

Galison, Peter. *Image and Logic: A Material Culture of Microphysics.* Chicago: U of Chicago P, 1997. Print.

Gere, Anne Ruggles. *Writing Groups: History, Theory, and Implications.* Carbondale: Southern Illinois UP, 1987. Print.

Geisler, Cheryl. "Literacy and Expertise in the Academy." *Language and Learning across the Disciplines* 1.1 (1994): 35–57. Print.

Gilbert, Martin. *The Holocaust: A History of the Jews in Europe during the Second World War.* New York: Holt, 1986. Print.

Glassick, Charles E., Mary T. Huber, and Gene I. Maeroff. *Scholarship Assessed: Evaluation of the Professoriate.* San Francisco: Jossey-Bass, 2003. Print.

Goldenberg, Myrna. "The Importance of Teaching the Holocaust in Community Colleges." *Testimony, Tensions and Tikkun: Teaching the Holocaust in Colleges and Universities.* Ed. Myrna Goldenberg and Rochelle L. Millen. Seattle: U of Washington P, 2007. 260–70. Print.

Goldhagen, Daniel Johah. *Hitler's Willing Executioners: Ordinary Germans and the Holocaust.* New York: Random House, 1996. Print.

Graff, Gerald. *Beyond the Culture Wars: How Teaching the Conflicts Can Revitalize American Education.* New York: Norton, 1993. Print.

Gross, Jan T. *Neighbors.* New York: Penguin, 2001. Print.

Heath, Shirley Brice. *Ways with Words: Language, Life, and Work in Classrooms and Communities.* New York: Cambridge UP, 1983. Print.

Hirsch, Marianne. "Surviving Images: Holocaust Photographs and the Work of Postmemory." *Visual Culture and the Holocaust.* Ed. Barbie Zelizer. New Brunswick, NJ: Rutgers UP, 2001. 215–46. Print.

Hirsch, Marianne, and Irene Kacandes, eds. *Teaching the Representation of the Holocaust.* New York: MLA, 2004. Print.

Hoffman, Eva. *After Such Knowledge: Memory, History, and the Legacy of the Holocaust.* New York: Public Affairs, 2004. Print.

Huber, Mary Taylor, and Pat Hutchings. "Situating the Scholarship of Teaching and Learning: A Cross-Disciplinary Conversation." *The Advancement of Learning: Building the Teaching Commons.* San Francisco: Jossey-Bass, 2005. 1–23. Print.

Huber, Mary Taylor, and Sherwyn P. Morreale, eds. *Disciplinary Styles in the Scholarship of Teaching and Learning: Exploring Common Ground.* Menlo Park, NJ: American Association for Higher Education and the Carnegie Foundation for the Advancement of Teaching, 2002. Print.

"Jablonka Koscielna: Podlaski." *International Jewish Cemetery Project.* International Association of Jewish Genealogical Societies, 28 May 2009. Web. 5 Mar. 2013.

Jay, Gregory. "Other People's Holocausts: Trauma, Empathy, and Justice in Anna Deavere Smith's *Fires in the Mirror.*" *Contemporary Literature* 48.1 (2001): 119–49. Web. 1 Aug. 2012.

"John S." *Fortunoff Video Archives for Holocaust Testimonies.* Yale U Library, 2009. Web. 1 Aug. 2012.

Katz, Steven T. "Jewish Faith after the Holocaust: Four Approaches." *The Holocaust: Readings and Interpretations.* Ed. Joseph R. Mitchell and Helen Buss Mitchell. New York: McGraw-Hill/Dushkin, 2011. 412–22. Print.

Katznelson, Ira. *Desolation and Enlightenment: Political Knowledge After Total War Totalitarianism and the Holocaust.* New York: Columbia UP, 2003. Print.

Kegan, Robert. *The Evolving Self.* Cambridge, MA: Harvard UP, 1982. Print.

———. *In Over Our Heads: The Mental Demands of Modern Life.* Cambridge, MA: Harvard UP, 1994. Print.

Klein, Julie Thompson. *Humanities, Culture, and Interdisciplinarity: The Changing American Academy,* Albany: State U of New York P, 2005. Print.

Langer, Lawrence. "The Alarmed Vision: Social Suffering and Holocaust Atrocity." *Daedalus* 125.1 (Winter 1996): 47–65. Print.

———, ed. *Art from the Ashes: A Holocaust Anthology.* New York: Oxford UP, 1995. Print.

———. "On Writing and Reading Holocaust Literature." *Art from the Ashes: A Holocaust Anthology.* Ed. Lawrence Langer. New York: Oxford UP, 1995. 3–9. Print.

Lenoir, Timothy. "The Discipline of Nature and the Nature of Disciplines." *Knowledges: Historical and Critical Studies in Disciplinarity.* Ed. Ellen Messer-Davidow, David R. Shumway, and David J. Sylvan. Charlottesville: UP of Virginia, 1993. 70–102. Print.

Levi, Primo. "Shame." *Art from the Ashes: A Holocaust Anthology.* Ed. Lawrence Langer. New York: Oxford UP, 1995. 108–18. Print.

Lewin, Abraham. "Diary of the Great Deportation." *Art from the Ashes: A Holocaust Anthology.* Ed. Lawrence Langer. New York: Oxford University Press, 1995. 161–96. Print.

Lewin, Ellis. "Camps." *Echoes and Reflection.* U of Southern California, n.d. Web. 9 Aug. 2012.

Lifton, Robert Jay. *Nazi Doctors: Medical Killing and the Psychology of Genocide.* New York: Basic, 1986. Print.

Lindquist, David H. "A Necessary Holocaust Pedagogy: Teaching the Teachers." *Issues in Teacher Education* 16.1 (Spring 2007): 21–36. Print.

Lipstadt, Deborah E. "Deniers, Relativists, and Pseudo-Scholarship." *The Holocaust: Readings and Interpretations*. Ed. Joseph R. Mitchell and Helen Buss Mitchell. New York: McGraw-Hill/Dushkin, 2001. 504–12. Print.

"Lvov." *United States Holocaust Memorial Museum*. U.S. Holocaust Memorial Museum, 2012. Web. 1 Aug. 2012.

Mansilla, Veronica Boix, and Elizabeth Dawes Duraising. "Targeted Assessment of Students' Interdisciplinary Work: An Empirically Grounded Framework Proposed." *Journal of Higher Education* 78.2 (Mar.–Apr. 2007): 215–37. Print.

Messer-Davidow, Ellen, David R. Shumway, and David J. Sylvan, eds. *Knowledges: Historical and Classical Studies in Disciplinarity*. Charlottesville: UP of Virginia, 1993. Print.

Messerschmidt, Kurt. "Kristallnacht." *Echoes and Reflections*. U of Southern California, n.d. Web. 1 Aug. 2012.

Mitchell, Joseph R., and Mitchell, Helen Buss "The Holocaust and the Jewish Covenant." *The Holocaust: Readings and Interpretations*. Ed. Joseph R. Mitchell and Helen Buss Mitchell. New York: McGraw-Hill/Dushkin, 2001. 411–12. Print.

———, eds. *The Holocaust: Readings and Interpretations*. New York: McGraw-Hill/Dushkin. 2001. Print.

Morrissette, Alana M. "The Experiences of Women during the Holocaust." *Jewish Heritage Centre of Western Canada*. Jewish Heritage Centre of Western Canada, 2004. Web. 1 Aug. 2012.

Niewyk, Donald L. ed. *The Holocaust: Problems and Perspectives of Interpretation*. Boston: Houghton-Mifflin, 2003. Print.

Nowacek, Rebecca. *Agents of Integration: Understanding Transfer as a Rhetorical Act*. Carbondale: Southern Illinois UP, 2011. Print.

Olère, David. *Unable to Work. A Teacher's Guide to the Holocaust*. U of South Florida, 2005. Web. 14 Aug. 2012.

Pagis, Dan. "Draft of a Reparations Agreement." *Art from the Ashes: A Holocaust Anthology*. Ed. Lawrence Langer. New York: Oxford UP, 1995. 592. Print.

Perry, William, Jr. *Forms of Intellectual and Ethical Development*. New York: Holt, Rinehart, and Winston. 1970. Print.

Piaget, Jean. *The Construction of Reality in the Child*. New York: Basic, 1956. Print.

Porat, Dan. *The Boy: A Holocaust Story*. New York: Hill and Wang, 2010. Print.

Rieff, David. "A Vast Choir of Voices." *The Nation* 249 (July 2012): 35–36, 38–42. Print.

Ross, Steven. "Steven Ross: Holocaust Survivor." Apr. 2011. Bristol Community College, Fall River, MA. Public presentation.

Rozett, Robert. "Fragments of Memory, The Faces behind the Documents, Artifacts and Photographs: The Central Theme for Holocaust Martyrs' and Heroes' Remembrance Day 2011." *Yad Vashem*. Web. April 2011.

Shakespeare, William. *Romeo and Juliet: New Variorum Edition*. Ed. Horace Howard Furness. New York: Dover, 1871. Print.

Shulman, Lee S. Foreword. *Disciplinary Styles in the Scholarship of Teaching and Learning*. Ed. Mary Taylor Huber and Sherwyn P. Morreale. Menlo Park, CA: American Association for Higher Education and the Carnegie Foundation for the Advancement of Teaching, 2002. v–ix. Print.

————. *Teaching as Community Property: Essays on Higher Education*. San Francisco: Jossey-Bass, 2004. Print.

Singer, Isaac Bashevis. "The Spinoza of Market Street." *The Collected Stories of Isaac Bashevis Singer*. New York: Farrar, 1953. 79–93. Print.

Spiegelman, Art. "Making of Maus: Interviewing Vladek." *Metamaus: The Complete Maus File*. New York: Pantheon, 2011. DVD-ROM.

————. *Maus I: A Survivor's Tale: My Father Bleeds History*. New York: Pantheon, 1986. Print.

————. *Maus II: A Survivor's Tale: And Here My Troubles Began*. New York: Pantheon, 1991. Print.

Sterling, Eric. "Indifferent Accomplices." *The Holocaust: Readings and Interpretations*. Ed. Joseph R. Mitchell and Helen Buss Mitchell. New York: McGraw-Hill/Dushkin, 2001. 183–92. Print.

Sternglass, Marilyn. *Time to Know Them: A Longitudinal Study of Writing and Learning at the College Level*. Mahwah, NJ: Lawrence Erlbaum, 1997. Print.

Sundstein, Bonnie. "Culture on the Page: Experience, Rhetoric, and Aesthetics in Ethnographic Writing." *Ethics and Representation in Qualitative Studies of Literacy*. Ed. Peter Mortensen Peter and Gesa E. Kirsch. Urbana, IL: National Council of Teachers of English, 1996. 177–201. Print.

"Tarnow." *Holocaust Encyclopedia*. U.S. Holocaust Memorial Museum, 6 Jan. 2001. Web. 27 July 2011.

Tinberg, Howard. "'Read As If for Life': What Happens When Students Encounter the Literature of the Shoah." *College Composition and Communication* 60.3 (2009): W1–17. Web. 24 June 2012.

Tinberg, Howard, and Ron Weisberger. Correspondence. 13 Aug. 2012. E-mail.

Tinberg, Sophie. Personal interview. Nov. 1994. DVD-ROM.

United States Census Bureau. "Fall River: Quick Facts." *State and County Quick Facts*. U.S. Census Bureau. 16 Aug. 2012. Web. 23 Aug. 2012.

Vess, Deborah, and Sherry Linkon. "Navigating the Interdisciplinary Archipelago: The Scholarship of Interdisciplinary Teaching and Learning." *Disciplinary Styles in the Scholarship of Teaching and Learning: Exploring Common Ground*. Menlo Park, NJ: Carnegie Foundation, 2002. 87–106. Print.

Wajsbord, Arie. "Jablonka, My Shtetl." Trans. Ada Holtzman. *Wysokie-Mazowieckie; Memorial Book Poland*. Museum of Jewish Heritage, 2011. Web. 26 July 2011.

Wasserstein, Bernard. *On the Eve: The Jews of Europe Before World War II*. New York: Simon and Schuster, 2012. Print.

Weiss, John. "The Ideology of Death." *The Holocaust: Readings and Interpretations*. Ed. Joseph R. Mitchell and Helen Buss Mitchell. New York: McGraw-Hill/Dushkin, 2011. 206–17. Print.

"Wöbbelin." *United States Holocaust Memorial Museum*. U.S. Holocaust Memorial Museum, 2012. Web. 1 Aug. 2012.

Wyman, David. *The Abandonment of the Jews: America and the Holocaust 1941–1945*. 2nd ed. New York: New P, 1998. Print.

Young, James E. "Between History and Memory: The Uncanny Voices of Historian and Survivor." *The Holocaust: Readings and Interpretations*. Ed. Joseph R. Mitchell and Helen Buss Mitchell. New York: McGraw-Hill/Dushkin, 2001. 532–41. Print.

INDEX

abstract generalization, 50
Abzug, Robert H., 20
Adorno, Theodor, 98
agents, 59, 60. *See also* bystanders
Appelfeld, Aharon, 38, 45, 85–86
Arendt, Hannah E., 21
Attleboro, MA, 22
Auschwitz, 6, 52, 63–65, 68–69, 87–88

Baeck, Leo, Rabbi, 91
Bak, Samuel, 37, 101
"banality of evil," 21
Bartov, Omer, 71
Bartrop, Paul R., 10
Bass, Randy, 3
Bauer, Yehuda, 9, 20, 47
Baxter-Magolda, Marcia, 49
Belenky, Mary Field, 49
Bergen, Doris L., 99
Berkovitz, Elizear, 93
Bernard-Donals, Michael, 20, 47, 52
Berthoff, Ann E., 27
"Between History and Memory: The
   Uncanny Voices of Historian and
   Survivor" (Young), 63
Blake, William, 89
Botwinick, Rita Steinhardt, 27, 29, 44
Boyer, Ernest L., ix
Brandeis University, 16
Brandt, Deborah, 6
Bristol Community College: disci-
   plines, integrating at, 25–39; history
   of, 21–22; honors program at, 7,
   23–24, 76; student demographics of,
   22–23; Tinberg narrative and, 11–17;
   Weisberger narrative and, 17–21
Bristol County, MA, 22
Britton, James, 6
Browning, Christopher, 100

bystanders: in camps, 59–60; engagement of, 52–53; in ghettos, 56–59;
   meaning of, 51; remaining as, 53–60

cannibalism, 72
Carnegie Academy for the Scholarship
   of Teaching and Learning (CASTL),
   xii
Carroll, James, 47
Catholic Church. *See* Roman Catholic
   Church
Chiseri-Strater, Elizabeth, 21
Chutzpah (Dershowitz), 11
"cognitive advancement," 34
College: The Undergraduate Experience
   (Boyer), ix
Commonwealth Honors Program
   (CHP) at Bristol Community College,
   7, 23–24, 76
community colleges: disciplines, characteristics of, 25–26; disciplines,
   integrating at, 33–37. *See also* Bristol
   Community College
"concrete facts," 50
contexts, institutional at Bristol
   Community College, 21–24
contexts, personal: Tinberg narrative as,
   11–17; Weisberger narrative as, 17–21
course structure: faculty contributions
   to, 40–42; goals of, 3–4; midterm and
   final exams and, 123–24; process of
   creation of, 44–49; research projects
   and, 119–22; student contributions,
   42–44; syllabus and, 109–15
Cushman, Ellen, 6

"deep" memory, 62, 71, 73, 80–81, 96. *See
   also* memory
Delbo, Charlotte, 60, 80–81, 87, 96

"Deniers, Relativists, and Pseudo-Scholarship" (Lipstadt), 35
Dershowitz, Alan, 11
Diary of Anne Frank, 42
"Diary of the Great Deportation" (Lewin, Abraham), 2, 9, 35, 56, 78
disciplinary methods, 3, 4, 8, 25–26, 34, 103–104
disciplines: community college level and, 25–26; integrating, creating conducive conditions for, 33–36, 37–39; pedagogical differences and, 28–30; understanding of, 27–28
"durational memory," 65

Eichmann, Adolf, 20
Emig, Janet, 6
empathy as student response, 79–85
Engel, David, 45
Epstein, Helen, 13
Erikson, Erik, 49
Ethics (Spinoza), 52
exams: student examples from, 96–98; template for, 123–24

faculty contributions to course structure, 40–42
faculty learning adjustments, 102–107
faith: challenges to personal, 90–91; challenges to religious, 91–94; learning adjustments of faculty, 102–107; learning adjustments of students, 94–98
Fall River, MA, 22–23
Felman, Shoshana, 76, 87
Fink, Ida, 27–28, 34–35, 57–58, 78–79
Forward (newspaper), 18
Friedlander, Albert H., 45

Galison, Peter, 36
genocide, 24, 81, 100
Gere, Anne, 6
Gilbert, Martin, 20
Glassick, Charles E., xii
goals of course structure, 3–4
Goldberger, Nancy Rule, 49

Goldenberg, Myrna, 24, 76
Graff, Gerald, 104
"gray zone," 98
Great Depression, 32
Gross, Jan T., 9, 46–47, 62–63, 77, 94, 105

Heath, Shirley Brice, 6
Hirsch, Marianne, 14
historical documentation, 5, 46, 62, 63. *See also* testimony
historical fact. *See* testimony
Hitler, Adolf, 15, 53–54
Hoffman, Eva, 13–14, 41
Holocaust. *See* Shoah (course); Shoah (event); *Shoah* (film)
Holocaust, The: Problems and Perspectives in Interpretation (Niewyk), 45
Holocaust, The: Readings and Interpretations (Mitchell), 47
Holocaust, The: The Third Reich and the Jews (Engel), 45
honors program. *See* Commonwealth Honors Program (CHP)
Huber, Mary T., xii, 32

"Ideology of Death, The" (Weiss), 54
Institute for Open Education, 17
integrated learning, 31–34
"integrated thinkers," 33–34

Jablonka (village in Poland), 12–13
Jedwabne (town in Poland), 63, 77, 94
Jewish Cemetery, Lvov, 80

Katz, Steven T., 91
Katznelson, Ira, 20–21
Kegan, Robert, 49–50
"Key Game, The" (Fink), 27–28, 57
Kindertransport, 44
Krakow, 12, 56
Kristallnacht, 55

Landsteiner, Bonnie, 6–7
Langer, Lawrence, 9, 30, 47, 65, 94–95
Lanzmann, Claude, 59
Lenoir, Timothy, 3–4

Levi, Primo, 60, 81–83, 98
Lewin, Abraham, 2, 9, 35, 38, 56–58, 78–79, 88
Lewin, Ellis, 68–69
Life is Beautiful (film), 43
Lindquist, David H., 41, 44
Linkon, Sherry, 1, 3, 4
Lipstadt, Deborah, 35–36
Lodz Ghetto, 52
Lunecki prison, 80
Lvov (town in Poland), 80

Maeroff, Gene I., xii
Maus (Spiegelman), 29–30, 46–47, 72, 83–84, 87–88, 105
Maybaum, Ignatz, 92–93
memory: "durational," 65; frailty of, 68, 89; intersection with historical record and, 5, 123; "memory work," 1, 9, 64
Messerschmidt, Kurt, 55–56, 66–68
metacognition, 27, 48, 84
methods of teaching/learning: disciplinary, 3, 4, 8, 25–26, 34, 103–104; traditional, 32, 37
midterm and final exams: student examples from, 96–98; template for, 123–24
Minsk Ghetto, 100
Mitchell, Helen, 47
Mitchell, Joseph, 47
Morreale, Sherwyn P., 32
"mystery of trauma," 75, 76, 87

National Socialist Party, 32. *See also* Nazis
Nazis, 13, 27, 38, 53–55, 66–69
Neighbors (Gross), 9, 46, 62, 77, 94, 97–98, 105
New Bedford, MA, 22–23
New Historicism, 29
Niewyk, Donald L., 45
Night (Wiesel), 21, 101
Nowacek, Rebecca, 32, 33–34
Nuremberg trials, 20, 62

Out of the Ashes: A Holocaust Anthology (Langer), 45

Out of the Whirlwind: A Reader of Holocaust Literature (Friedlander), 45

Pagis, Dan, 37, 98
"pedagogies of interruption," 2
Perry, William, Jr., 49
personal contexts: Tinberg narrative as, 11–17; Weisberger narrative as, 17–21
Piaget, Jean, 49
Porat, Dan, 40–41

rape, 72–74
reading journals: student examples, 52–60, 63–64, 66, 73, 78, 82, 84–89, 92–94; template for, 117–18
relativism, 35–36
re-learning process: by faculty, 102–107; by students, 94–98
"Remembering the Holocaust in Literature and History" (course description), 1, 23, 26, 31
research project and course structure, 119–22
rhetorical processes, 25–26
Roman Catholic Church, 6, 47
Ross, Steven, 71–74, 96
Rubenstein, Richard, 93

S., John (Jesuit priest), 69–71
Sach, Nelly, 98
Schindler's List (film), 21, 42–43, 78
Scholarship of Teaching and Learning (SoTL), ix–xii, 17, 20
Scholarship Reconsidered (Boyer), ix
Shoah (course): creation process of, 44–49; goals of, 3–4; midterm and final exam template, 123–24; research project and, 119–22; student contributions to, 42–44; syllabus, 109–15
Shoah (event): denial of, 6, 35–36; representations of by students, 98–102
Shoah (film), 59–60
Shulman, Lee S., 1–2, 3, 7, 25
Singer, Isaac Bashevis, 52
social constructionist framework, 49–50
Sonderkommandos, 59

SoTL. *See* Scholarship of Teaching and Learning (SoTL)
Sounds of Silence (Bak), 101
Spiegelman, Art, 29–30, 46–47, 72, 83–84, 87–88, 98, 105
Spinoza, Baruch, 52
"Spinoza of Market Street, The" (Singer), 52
"Spring Morning, A" (Fink), 34, 57–58, 78
Sternglass, Marilyn, 6
student contributions to course structure, 42–44
student learning adjustments, 94–98
student projects, 98–102
survivors. *See* testimony
syllabus of course structure, 109–15

Tarnow (city in Poland), 12–13
Tarule, Jill Mattock, 49
teaching as a scholarly activity: methods used, 6–7; pedagogically based questions about, 1–3; points of inquiry about, 3–6
Teaching English at the Two-Year College (journal), xi, xii
teaching styles, integration of, 31–37
Tek, Nechama, 47
Terezin, 91
testimony: audio/video, in, 9, 61, 69–71; durational memory and, 65–66; effects on students, 80; empathy and, 79–85; importance of, 90, 96, 99; as memory work expression, 64–65; problems with, 89; survivors and, 9, 48, 61–62, 71–74, 82; use of for students, 55, 57, 63; as witness, 9, 36, 55, 63–64, 66–69
Theresienstadt, 91

Third Reich, 29, 62
Tinberg, Howard, 11–17
traditional methods, 32, 37
trauma and *Shoah* studies: critiquing from a distance, 85–89; empathy and, 79–85; personal struggles with, 76–77; student responses to, handling of, 77–79. *See also* "mystery of trauma"
Treaty of Versailles, 32, 53
Tzili (Appelfeld), 38, 85–87, 98

Ukrainians, 80
United States Memorial Holocaust Museum, 48, 100
University of Southern California Shoah Foundation, 48
University Without Walls, 17
unlearning, lessons in, 103–107

Vess, Deborah, 1, 3, 4
"Voices" (Delbo), 80–81

Warsaw, 52–53, 56
Warsaw Ghetto, 35, 38, 52, 78–79, 88
Wasersztajn, Szmul, 62–63, 77
Wasserstein, Bernard, 40
Weisberger, Ronald, 17–21
Weiss, John, 54
Wiesel, Elie, 21, 53, 101
witness testimony. *See* testimony
witnesses: integrated course and, 61–63; seeing and yet unseen, 69–71; as spectacle, 71–74; role of testimony, 63–66
World War I, 27, 32, 53
World War II, 12, 20–21
Wyman, David, 20

yiddishkeit, 16
Young, James E., 63–65

HOWARD TINBERG is Professor of English at Bristol Community College. He is author of three books: *Border Talk: Writing and Knowing in the Two-Year College; Writing with Consequence: What Writing Does in the Disciplines;* and (with Jean-Paul Nadeau) *The Community College Writer: Exceeding Expectations.* He is editor, with Patrick Sullivan, of *What Is "College-Level" Writing?* and, with Patrick Sullivan and Sheridan Blau, of *What Is "College-Level" Writing? II.* Tinberg is 2004 Carnegie/CASE Community Colleges Professor of the Year and served as a Carnegie Scholar in 2005–2006.

RONALD WEISBERGER has been Coordinator of Tutoring at Bristol Community College in Fall River, Massachusetts, since 1985. He is also Adjunct Professor of History and teaches courses on world history, American history, and African American history. He has published articles on the history of higher education, teaching and learning, adult development, and developmental education.

CPSIA information can be obtained at www.ICGtesting.com
Printed in the USA
LVOW07s0701080416

482624LV00006BA/249/P